Internships
in Psychology

Internships
in Psychology

The APAGS Workbook
for Writing Successful Applications
and Finding the Right Fit

Fourth Edition

Carol Williams-Nickelson

Mitchell J. Prinstein

W. Gregory Keilin

AMERICAN PSYCHOLOGICAL ASSOCIATION
Washington, DC

Published by
American Psychological Association
750 First Street, NE
Washington, DC 20002
www.apa.org

APA Order Department
P.O. Box 92984
Washington, DC 20090-2984
Phone: (800) 374-2721; Direct: (202) 336-5510
Fax: (202) 336-5502; TDD/TTY: (202) 336-6123
Online: http://www.apa.org/pubs/books
E-mail: order@apa.org

In the U.K., Europe, Africa, and the Middle East, copies may be ordered from
Eurospan Group
c/o Turpin Distribution
Pegasus Drive
Stratton Business Park
Biggleswade, Bedfordshire
SG18 8TQ United Kingdom
Phone:+44 (0) 1767 604972
Fax: +44 (0) 1767 601640
Online: https://www.eurospanbookstore.com/apa
E-mail: eurospan@turpin-distribution.com

Typeset in Trump Mediaeval by Circle Graphics, Inc., Columbia, MD

Printer: Sheridan Books, Chelsea, MI
Cover Designer: Naylor Design, Washington, DC

Library of Congress Cataloging-in-Publication Data

Names: Williams-Nickelson, Carol, author. | Prinstein, Mitchell J., 1970-author. |
  Keilin, W. Gregory, author.
Title: Internships in psychology : the APAGS workbook for writing successful
  applications and finding the right fit / by Carol Williams Nickelson,
  Mitchell J. Prinstein, and W. Gregory Keilin.
Description: Fourth Edition. | Washington, DC : American Psychological
  Association, [2019] | Revised edition of the authors' Internships in
  psychology, c2013. | Includes bibliographical references and index.
Identifiers: LCCN 2018008940 (print) | LCCN 2018013515 (ebook) | ISBN
  9781433829598 (ebook) | ISBN 1433829592 (ebook) | ISBN 9781433829581 |
  ISBN 9781433829581 (print) | ISBN 1433829584 (print)
Subjects: LCSH: Psychology—Study and teaching (Internship)
Classification: LCC BF77 (ebook) | LCC BF77 .I67 2019 (print) | DDC
  150.71/55—dc23
LC record available at https://lccn.loc.gov/2018008940

British Library Cataloguing-in-Publication Data
A CIP record is available from the British Library.

Printed in the United States of America
Fourth Edition

http://dx.doi.org/10.1037/0000102-000

10 9 8 7 6 5 4 3 2 1

In Memoriam

Shane J. Lopez, PhD
1970–2016

We dedicate this edition of the workbook in memoriam of our dear friend and colleague, Shane J. Lopez. Shane's many contributions to earlier editions of this workbook, his participation in many of our American Psychological Association preconvention workshops, his national leadership on behalf of students and the American Psychological Association of Graduate Schools, and his effortless good humor will always be remembered and appreciated. We look back on the many years we knew Shane with fondness and tremendous gratitude for the person he was and for the ways he enriched our lives, both personally and professionally. We deeply miss our friend, but his message of hope lives on in the hearts and deeds of countless others.

CONTENTS

PREFACE

Not so long ago, few resources were available to help students navigate the internship application process. Students experienced a great deal of anxiety and confusion throughout the process and had many questions about how best to proceed. This great unmet need led the three of us to become involved with local and national associations that advocate for students and attend to training issues. We served on committees, were elected to offices, and were asked to speak at conferences about the internship process. These activities ultimately led to the creation of the first American Psychological Association of Graduate Students (APAGS) special preconvention workshop on the internship application process, which was presented at the 108th Annual Convention of the American Psychological Association (APA) in 2000 in Washington, DC.

We created a set of handouts, which we conceived as a workbook, that were designed to help applicants prepare for each aspect of the internship application process in a careful, systematic manner. We hoped that through the workshop and the workbook, we would help students reconsider the internship application process as an opportunity to start establishing their professional identity by consulting with advisors, developing professional goals, meeting dozens of professionals with a range of experiences, and discussing their professional development and interests with people outside of their graduate program. By reframing the tasks involved in this process, we hoped that the application procedure might become a little less cumbersome and that applicants could focus on finding not just *any* internship but the *right* internship for them.

The workshop was a hit, and our hopes for this workbook were more than realized. The early versions of this workbook were distributed directly by the APAGS office and were very well-received. We were therefore happy when, in 2004, APA Books took over publication of the workbook and gave it even wider distribution. Our goal has always been to help students get through a process that can seem daunting and even confusing because of all the advice—good and not-so-good—circulating in programs.

This is our fourth edition of the workbook, reflecting ongoing changes in the application process and trends in psychology training and internship availability. The application process is now an online system. The process known as the Clearinghouse has been replaced by Phase II of the Match and the Post-Match Vacancy Service. There is now a Standardized Reference Form. And, perhaps most important, the internship marketplace has changed dramatically. This edition of the workbook offers updated and enhanced information to address the evolution and many modifications to the application process. In recent years, we added a chapter for directors of clinical training, offering suggestions on how they might best assist students during this process. Numerous additional changes also have been made—many of which are based on readers' feedback on earlier editions.

We are pleased that the workbook is now available to a greater number of students and that APA Books shares our goal of keeping the price low to accommodate students' limited budgets. Since our first APAGS workshop 18 years ago, we have donated all our royalties from prior workshop registration fees and workbook sales to APAGS to continue supporting programs that directly benefit students. For example, in earlier years, some of us have presented portions of the internship workshop around the country for APAGS, and sales of the book have supported many APAGS scholarships and awards, additional APAGS-developed programs that address internship issues, and other important aspects of graduate training in psychology. Thus, we receive no direct financial gain from our work on this project. Our reward is knowing that we are helping you! We are thrilled that readers have found this workbook to be an invaluable resource, and we are very pleased to offer this new edition with substantial changes and updates.

Similar to past editions, this volume has a practical orientation, presenting a discussion of each aspect of the internship process in order and with new insights. We have included numerous examples to help applicants calculate their clinical hours, compose essays, craft impressive cover letters, write thank-you notes, and practice interview questions. The examples are from real applicants, all of whom successfully obtained an internship match; they are neither ideal nor flawless but are realistic, excellent examples that illustrate many of the suggestions offered in this volume. We are grateful to the generous and courageous applicants who provided us with their materials to be presented anonymously in this book.

We hope this volume will continue to provide readers the support, assistance, and perspective they need to successfully navigate the internship application process.

Good luck to you all!

ACKNOWLEDGMENTS

This is for you, internship applicants! Because of your consistent positive feedback over the years, we have remained committed to helping you achieve success throughout the internship process. This workbook was developed to address your needs and was shaped by your feedback and encouragement during our annual American Psychological Association of Graduate Students (APAGS) internship workshops and other conversations. Your ongoing support and expressions of gratitude have been our inspiration and the motivating force for both completing this project and keeping the content fresh and relevant. Your membership in APAGS has also helped to make our workshop and workbook available to students each year. We hope this workbook offers you some direction, comfort, and perspective, along with a little humor, throughout the internship application process.

We also thank all the students who voluntarily provided sections of their actual internship application materials for use in this workbook without any expectation of recognition or reward. Their gesture of camaraderie is greatly appreciated because their work will help future generations of internship applicants.

We also gratefully acknowledge Richard Suinn, past president of the American Psychological Association (APA), and the APA Board of Directors for allocating seed money from their limited contingency funds in 2000 to help launch the workshop and workbook. Nadine J. Kaslow, past chair of the Association of Psychology Postdoctoral and Internship Centers (APPIC), and the entire APPIC board deserve tremendous recognition for their dedication to students and to internship training.

Carol Williams-Nickelson thanks the staff of the University of Notre Dame Counseling Center, especially Sue Steibe-Pasalich, Patrick Utz, Micky Franco, Rita Donley, and Dominic Vachon, for a memorable and richly rewarding internship experience. The immeasurable support provided by her colleagues at APA, particularly L. Michael Honaker, her former boss and mentor, and former deputy chief executive officer of APA, is deeply appreciated. Carol is grateful to her husband, David Nickelson, JD, PsyD, for his encouragement in all her endeavors. Most important, Carol thanks her precious daughters, Jillian and Tiffany, for excusing their mom to participate in seemingly endless APA meetings and for being the youngest budding psychologists to attend the internship workshop (Jillian at less than 2 months old in Louisville, Kentucky, in March 2005 and Tiffany at 11 months old in San Francisco, California, in August 2007).

Mitch Prinstein extends unending gratitude to his mentors, Annette La Greca and Tony Spirito, for their career guidance and support, as well as to Audrey Zakriski, Greta Francis, Fran D'Elia, Rod Gragg, and Donn Posner for an excellent internship experience. Mitch also extends thanks to his friends and family for everything, always.

Greg Keilin thanks his graduate advisor, Scott Hamilton, and his internship training director, Melba Vasquez, for their support and mentorship throughout the years. He also thanks his colleagues on the APPIC Board of Directors, an incredibly energetic and dedicated group of individuals who have been willing to take the bold steps necessary to support quality training and to make the internship selection process more manageable for students.

Internships
in Psychology

1 GETTING STARTED: GENERAL OVERVIEW OF THE INTERNSHIP APPLICATION PROCESS

The psychology internship application process can be rewarding, exhausting, stressful, and exciting. Your internship training marks the beginning of the final stages of your graduate career in professional psychology and is a milestone that you should be proud of reaching. Congratulations!

You have been preparing for internship since your first day of graduate school. As a result, you have acquired many valuable experiences that can make you very attractive to the right internship program. The process of gathering materials, calculating your clinical hours, developing your curriculum vitae (CV), establishing and articulating your internship and career goals, interviewing with various internship sites, being matched to a site that is a good fit, and finally going on internship is one of the most valuable exercises you will undertake as a graduate student. This process will help you review and assess all of your previous training, evaluate your collective graduate experiences, define your training and career goals, practice your job application and interviewing skills, and launch you into your career as a psychologist.

This chapter provides you with a broad overview of the entire internship application process and gives you some organizational tools to assist you in preparation. It is no secret that decisions about internship often are difficult and anxiety provoking. The process includes many unknown factors that you may be contemplating: Where will I go? Will I measure up? Will my application be competitive? Do I really have what it takes to make it? Can I move? Will I survive living in a region that has snow? Will my family be supportive? How will I live on my small stipend? What will my supervisors be like? Will I connect with my fellow interns? What will be next for me after internship? Will I have a positive experience? As you well know, change is rarely easy and is almost always stressful. We hope to help you to eliminate some of the unproductive worry you

http://dx.doi.org/10.1037/0000102-001
Internships in Psychology: The APAGS Workbook for Writing Successful Applications and Finding the Right Fit, Fourth Edition, by C. Williams-Nickelson, M. J. Prinstein, and W. G. Keilin

may be experiencing and instead to capitalize on the normal, productive, and motivating anxiety that is a natural part of doing anything new and different, particularly when you are being evaluated. So, relax as much as you can and do your best to learn from and enjoy this process.

We understand that you may be worried about the many nuances of where and how to apply for internships and especially how to present yourself to an entirely new group of faculty and supervisors who will be evaluating you all over again. Although you have probably already established yourself in your doctoral program as a competent student with a variety of talents, soon you will be faced with the task of explaining and demonstrating your competence and interests to a new group of evaluators. This is not the first time that you will have to do this, nor will it be the last. Each time you apply for a new job, even if you have a stellar and well-known reputation, you will have to sell yourself and your skills. Preparing for and applying to internship sites is one of the best ways of practicing for future job interviews and opportunities. If you plan and prepare well now, you will gain valuable skills and knowledge that will benefit you for years to come.

THE PREDOCTORAL INTERNSHIP

The psychology predoctoral internship is typically a year-long, full-time clinical training experience that is a required part of a student's doctoral program. The internship is often described as the "capstone" of graduate training in psychology and differs from practicum and work experience by its rigorous nature, its timing in the overall sequence of graduate training, the intensive supervision and training received, the focus on the development of advanced skills, and the high level of organization and commitment to the training program that is required of the sponsoring agency. Although a very limited number of 2-year, half-time internship positions are available, the vast majority of students attend internship on a full-time basis. The internship typically occurs in the final year of one's doctoral program and ideally after the student has completed comprehensive examinations and proposed (or, it is hoped, defended) his or her dissertation. The policies of the Association of Psychology Postdoctoral and Internship Centers (APPIC) state that internship applicants must be currently enrolled in a doctoral program in health service psychology (i.e., clinical, counseling, or school psychology or some combination of those three areas) that requires internship training and must have completed practicum experience.

Applicants begin preparing for internship at the beginning of their training programs by carefully selecting the type of practicum training they receive and by tracking and recording all related training hours, experiences, and supervision. This process helps prospective interns consider the type of training they still need when it comes time to apply for internship.

ASSOCIATION OF PSYCHOLOGY POSTDOCTORAL AND INTERNSHIP CENTERS

The first step in preparing for internship is to become familiar with APPIC and its website (http://www.appic.org). APPIC is the organization that oversees many aspects of psychology internship and postdoctoral training in the United States and Canada, most notably the selection and placement of interns and postdoctoral fellows. APPIC is governed by a board of directors that is elected by its membership—nearly 1,000 internship and postdoctoral training programs in the United States and Canada.

It is important to understand that APPIC is not an accrediting body; it is a membership organization. In other words, an internship program that is a member of APPIC may or may not be accredited. Accreditation is granted by other organizations, as we discuss in the next section. You may occasionally hear someone mistakenly refer to an internship program as "APPIC accredited" when they really likely mean that the program is an APPIC member.

To become and remain an APPIC member, an internship program must meet APPIC's membership criteria. Although these criteria have been developed to be indicators of quality training, they are not as rigorous, comprehensive, or highly regarded as the standards used by recognized accrediting organizations in psychology. Furthermore, the review process to become an APPIC member (submitting a written application that is reviewed by a committee) involves far less scrutiny than does the process of attaining accreditation.

APPIC oversees the internship selection process and provides a number of services and resources for prospective interns, doctoral programs, and internship programs, such as

- the *APPIC Directory Online*, which is a catalog of APPIC-member internship programs that is searchable using a variety of criteria;
- the APPIC Application for Psychology Internships (AAPI) Online service (pronounced "app-ee"), a service that allows students to develop a standardized application that can be submitted to multiple internship sites via the Internet;
- the APPIC Match, an organized and fair process by which students are placed into internship positions based on the expressed preferences of applicants and programs;
- the APPIC Post-Match Vacancy Service, a process that operates after the APPIC Match has completed, connecting students who remain unmatched with programs that have unfilled positions;
- informal problem consultation and a formal complaint process, services to assist students who run into difficulties during the application/selection process or while on internship; and
- extensive information, statistics, FAQs, e-mail lists, and other resources to assist students and programs in navigating the internship application and selection experiences.

We discuss these services and resources in greater detail in the chapters that follow.

WHAT IS ACCREDITATION? In a nutshell, an accredited program is one that has met certain standards of quality as defined by an accrediting body. Accreditation is a voluntary process that is rigorous, time consuming, and expensive for a program to attain. Internship programs that apply for accreditation usually develop an organized training model along with a sequence of training and clinical experiences that fit that model. They must provide a certain level of supervision, adequate physical resources, and a reasonable stipend. Furthermore, every 5 to 10 years, internship programs must complete an extensive document called a Self-Study (which is usually longer than a dissertation!) and host an intensive, multiday, on-site visit by representatives of the accrediting body.

Currently, two organizations are generally recognized and accepted as accrediting bodies in psychology: the American Psychological Association (APA) for programs in the United States, and the Canadian Psychological Association (CPA) for programs in Canada. A program that is accredited by APA or CPA has achieved the highest form of recognition available. Students who complete APA- or CPA-accredited doctoral and internship programs are least likely to have difficulties in becoming licensed or in securing employment as a psychologist.

Accreditation by APA and CPA is different from other forms of accreditation (e.g., regional accreditation) because those other forms carry very little weight when it comes to your future as a psychologist. For the purposes of this workbook, the term *accreditation* refers only to accreditation by APA or CPA.

You may be surprised to hear that according to APA, psychology is the only major health profession that does not require its students to attend accredited doctoral and internship programs to be qualified to practice. In recent years, many have argued that this situation is both unjustifiable and unsustainable, given the importance of ensuring the provision of high-quality services to clients/patients, as well as the need for psychologists to be seen as competent and qualified in an increasingly integrated health care environment.

In fact, things are changing rapidly when it comes to the importance of accreditation within psychology. In 2013, the APA Council of Representatives approved a resolution that stated that health service psychologists must be trained in accredited doctoral and internship programs and further identified a timeline for the implementation of these standards. Although this resolution reflects only APA's official perspective on the matter, it has had great influence since it was approved. For example, there has been a significant effort to assist internship programs in the accreditation process; in early 2018, approximately 80% (630 out of nearly 800) of internships that were APPIC members were also accredited, a substantial increase from just a few years earlier. Furthermore, some licensing boards have already enacted rules that require a candidate to have graduated from an accredited doctoral program or internship to be licensed.

Although no one can predict the future with certainty, from our perspective it seems very likely that accreditation will soon become the standard for education and training in psychology, and virtually all students will graduate from accredited doctoral programs and complete accredited internships. This suggests that those who have completed nonaccredited training programs will find themselves more and more in the minority, facing increased competition, fewer opportunities, and some doors being closed entirely.

Attending an accredited internship can help you feel confident that you will have a high-quality training experience as well as the comfort of knowing that it is highly unlikely that you will encounter barriers when applying for licensure or employment. On the other hand, if you are considering attending a nonaccredited internship program, it is important that you understand the potential risks in doing so. Some jurisdictions have specific criteria that an unaccredited internship must meet for the candidate to be licensed. If your internship does not meet those requirements, you will not be able to be licensed as a psychologist in that jurisdiction (see the Association of State and Provincial Psychology Boards' website at http://www.asppb.org for more information). As far as future employment is concerned, many employers explicitly state that they will only employ psychologists who interned at and/or graduated from accredited programs. Some examples of situations in which an accredited doctoral program and/or internship are more likely to be required of applicants include academic positions and faculty appointments, governmental agencies, hospitals and other medical facilities, positions located in certain competitive geographic regions (e.g., New York City), appointments to some managed-care panels, and all psychologist positions in Veterans Affairs hospitals and clinics.

So, what does all of this mean for you and your decisions about internship? For one thing, it means that, more than ever, you should consider nonaccredited internship programs only if you fully understand the risks. And, those risks should be considered with an eye toward the future—and the knowledge that what worked in the past for some may not work in the future. Specifically, if one of your mentors tells you not to worry about attending a nonaccredited internship, you should understand that such advice may be based on past experiences that have limited relevance to where psychology is heading. This advice may be provided in good faith, with a genuine desire to be helpful, but it also may not be accurate for today's graduate students. It is vitally important that you do your homework and talk to a variety of people in making this important decision. Remember, if you decide to accept a nonaccredited internship and eventually run into difficulties, there are currently almost no options to do a second (accredited) internship.

CHANGES IN APPIC MATCH ELIGIBILITY

Based on the changes taking place in the field related to accreditation, APPIC decided that a student would be eligible to participate in the Match and Post-Match Vacancy Service only if he or she was (a) enrolled in an accredited doctoral program, or (b) enrolled in a nonaccredited doctoral program that had reached the point in its accreditation process to have been awarded a site visit by an accrediting organization. This change took effect beginning with the 2017–2018 selection process for the 2018–2019 internship training year.

Although this change will not affect the vast majority of students, because most are from accredited doctoral programs, the 200+ students from nonaccredited programs who seek internship each year will be seriously affected. APPIC did announce what it described as a "one-year, one-time" partial exception for the 2018 Match, allowing students from nonaccredited doctoral programs to seek positions in the Post-Match Vacancy Service once both phases of the Match were over. However, as of this writing, APPIC had not yet determined whether it would extend that exception to future years. You should check the APPIC web site for the latest eligibility criteria.

If you are currently enrolled in a doctoral program that is not yet accredited, we strongly encourage you discuss your options with your director of clinical training. In particular, if your doctoral program is not in the process of seeking accreditation, you and your fellow students may wish to encourage them to do so.

INTERNSHIP SUPPLY AND DEMAND

You have probably heard much about the psychology internship supply-and-demand problem, which refers to the long-standing shortage of internship positions as compared with the number of applicants who are seeking such positions. And you may have witnessed students who were a few years ahead of you in your doctoral program going through the stress and worry of not matching, having to wait a year, and so on.

Fortunately, as of this writing, those issues have greatly diminished. The number of internship positions has increased markedly in the past few years, while the number of graduate students matriculating through psychology doctoral programs has decreased. In fact, the selection process for the 2017–2018 training year resulted in approximately 200 internship positions in the United States and Canada that were never filled. Thus, with rare exceptions, there is now an internship position for every psychology graduate student who wants one. Table 1.1 provides a comparison of the Match participation numbers between 2012 (the year of the worst imbalance) and 2017.

What remains, however, is a shortage of accredited internship positions, although that is rapidly improving as well. In the 2017 APPIC Match, there were 752 fewer accredited positions than the number of applicants, which meant that there were accredited positions for 81% of all applicants (as compared with an accredited position for 53% of applicants back in 2012).

These changes are terrific news for applicants and are the result of much effort (not to mention money) from the psychology education and training community. For you, it means that you will be able to avoid much of the angst and worry about not matching that was experienced by students who sought internship just a few years ago. However, it does not mean that you can submit mediocre applications to sites or not take the process seriously, and it remains important for you to devote sufficient time and effort to the process.

WHY DO SOME PEOPLE HAVE DIFFICULTY GETTING MATCHED TO A PREFERRED INTERNSHIP?

Here are some of the more common reasons that applicants have difficulty matching or don't match to one of their higher-ranked programs.

- *Applicant is geographically restricted.* Some applicants, because of family, financial, employment, or other obligations, are limited geographically in their internship search. This can result in an insufficient number of sites to which one can apply or being put in a position of applying to sites that are a poor fit for one's training needs. Although geographic restrictions are unavoidable for some, those who do have geographic flexibility are generally encouraged to broaden their search to prevent these difficulties.
- *Applicant applies to too few sites.* As outlined in Table 1.2, applying to fewer than 11 internship sites can result in a greater chance of remaining unmatched.
- *Applicant applies to primarily "competitive" sites (i.e., sites that receive a large number of applications for a small number of positions).* Some sites receive hundreds of applications, and those who apply exclusively to such sites run a greater risk of not matching—regardless of their qualifications.

Table 1.1. *Five-Year Comparison of APPIC Match Statistics (2012–2017)*

	2012	2017	5-year change	
Participating sites	703	782	+79	(+11%)
Positions offered	3,190	3,849	+659	(+21%)
Positions filled	2,968	3,197	+229	(+8%)
Positions unfilled	222	652	+430	(+194%)
Registered applicants	4,435	3,921	−514	(−12%)
Withdrawn applicants	426	266	−160	(−38%)
Matched applicants	2,968	3,197	+229	(+8%)
Unmatched applicants	1,041	458	−583	(−56%)

Note. Data from the official Association of Psychology Postdoctoral and Internship Centers (APPIC) Match Statistics from 2012 and 2017 (https://www.appic.org/Match/Match-Statistics). These numbers reflect activity from Phase I only.

Table 1.2. *Relationship Between Submitted Applications and Chances of Being Matched*

Number of applications submitted	2017 match rate
1–5	67%
6–10	79%
11–15	91%
16–20	92%
21 or more	88%

Note. Data from the 2017 Association of Psychology Postdoctoral and Internship Centers Post-Match Internship Survey of Applicants.

- *Applicant needs to attend a part-time internship.* Unfortunately, the number of 2-year, part-time psychology internship positions is far lower than the number of students who prefer them.
- *Applicant is from an unaccredited doctoral program.* As noted previously, accreditation is becoming an increasingly important factor in hiring decisions, and the internship process is no exception. Many internship programs will not accept students from nonaccredited doctoral programs.
- *Applicant is not a good fit for the programs to which he or she applies.* An extremely important part of the internship application process is to choose sites that are a good fit for your background, training, and experiences. Internship training directors often consider fit to be one of the most important criteria when evaluating applicants. Applying to more than a few sites that aren't a good fit for you can lower your chances of being matched.
- *Essays and/or cover letters are poorly written or not compelling.* Your essays and cover letters provide you with the opportunity to make your application truly come alive, and most applicants go through multiple drafts and get feedback from trusted mentors. Cover letters that are generic (i.e., not written and tailored to each site) are not viewed favorably by internship sites. Essays and cover letters will be addressed in later chapters.
- *Interviewing skills are deficient.* Just because you are a wonderful graduate student, a wonderful clinician, a wonderful researcher, and so on, doesn't necessarily mean that you interview well! In our experience, some of the most wonderful and qualified applicants simply don't present themselves well on an interview. Ask your faculty and mentors to do mock interviews with you, as that can go a long way in helping you develop those skills and present yourself to maximum advantage. We address this topic in Chapter 5.
- *Letters of recommendation are weak.* It is important that you have open and frank conversations with potential reference writers in advance about their willingness to write you a strong letter of recommendation. More information on this topic is in Chapter 4.

HOW MANY SITES SHOULD YOU APPLY TO?

Each year, many applicants wonder how many internship programs they should apply to in order to maximize their chances of being matched. Data from the 2017 APPIC Match showed that applicants submitted an average of 15.2 applications (SD = 5.5, Mdn = 15) in Phase I. Results from a 2016 APPIC post-Match survey indicated that applicants reported receiving an average of 7.2 interviews (SD = 4.0, Mdn = 7). See Table 1.2 for information about the relationship between the number of applications submitted and the likelihood of being successfully matched in 2017.

As you can see from this table, applying to more than 15 sites does not appear to improve your chances of being matched. We recommend applying to between 11 and 15 sites, and certainly no more than 15. Staying in this range enables you to keep the number of interviews at a manageable (both emotionally and financially) level and to avoid the significantly increased per-application cost that occurs beginning with the 16th application that you submit.

INTERNSHIP
MILESTONES

The internship application process can be long and arduous. Consider the process to be a series of small, manageable tasks. To help you review these tasks and ensure that you stay on track, consult the "Internship Milestones at a Glance" checklist (see Exhibit 1.1) throughout the application process. We encourage you to refer to this list often and record the dates on which you accomplish each milestone.

The more organized you are, the easier it will be to complete your applications and to meet the many overlapping deadlines. The suggested checklist can help you arrange all of your supporting application materials so that, when it is time, you can complete your application with minimal frustration and without scrambling for information. Obtaining and organizing the information you will need to report on the AAPI Online can be a long process, so you need to get started early.

Exhibit 1.1.   *Internship Milestones at a Glance*

1. Compute practicum hours, including anticipated hours.
2. Create an account for the AAPI Online service at http://www.appic.org.
3. Use the *APPIC Directory Online* to find sites that match your interests. Review each site's web-based materials or request their materials via e-mail. Keep notes about your impressions as well as application requirements and deadlines.
4. Register for the APPIC Match (see the Match website at http://www.natmatch.com/psychint).
5. Have your graduate transcripts sent to the AAPI Online service.
6. Prepare curriculum vitae.
7. Request reference letters (letter writers must use the Standardized Reference Form).
8. Draft application essays.
9. Write individual cover letters (and any site-specific supplemental materials) for each site to which you are applying.
10. Finish the AAPI Online and submit to your DCT for verification.
11. Submit completed applications to internship sites.
12. While waiting for interview offers, practice your interviewing skills, including mock orals with mentors and a sample case presentation.
13. Schedule interviews.
14. Prepare for interviews: review sites' materials, compose questions to ask, consider a literature search on those with whom you will interview (if appropriate).
15. Attend interviews.
16. Send thank-you notes/follow-up letters (optional).
17. Compose and submit Rank Order List for the Match before the deadline.

Note. AAPI = APPIC Application for Psychology Internships; APPIC = Association of Psychology Postdoctoral and Internship Centers; DCT = director of clinical training.

Here is how we recommend that you get started with the internship application process.

Step 1. Visit the APPIC Website

You should begin the process with a visit to the APPIC website (http://www.appic.org), with a focus on the three specific areas outlined below.

1a. *Review the AAPI Online.* Create a new account for the AAPI Online service (there is no charge to do so) and explore the various sections and requirements. Doing so well in advance will provide you with an important head start in terms of understanding the information that you will need to collect and enter into your online application. In fact, it is extremely helpful to maintain a log of your clinical experiences beginning with your very first (i.e., first- or second-year) graduate school practicum experience, as the AAPI Online asks for very extensive information (e.g., treatment setting, type of intervention, client demographics) about those experiences.

1b. *Search the APPIC Directory Online.* Most students find that the *APPIC Directory Online* is their most useful source of information on internship programs, as it lists the nearly 800 internship programs that are current APPIC members. The *APPIC Directory Online* is updated regularly by internship training directors and provides excellent search capabilities. Entering a set of search parameters and clicking the "Search" button will yield a list of internship programs that match your criteria. You may then click on any internship program in that list to display more information about that specific program. Note that a few APA divisions also maintain their own internship directories for programs that fit a specific area of interest (e.g., clinical neuropsychology; science-oriented internship programs) that are available online as well.

   Here are some tips on getting the most out of searching the *APPIC Directory Online:*

   - Before beginning your search, be sure you understand the requirements of your doctoral program when it comes to selecting an internship. Are you required to attend an accredited internship? If not, are there other requirements that internships must meet to be acceptable? Be sure you understand your doctoral program's requirements before proceeding with your search.
   - Be sure to check out the variety of search parameters that are available to you, as there are quite a few. Click on the "Search by Program Criteria" link on the search criteria page to expand the full range of search options.
   - You may specify as many or as few search parameters as you wish. Increasing the number of search parameters used generally decreases the number of internship programs returned by the search.
   - You may find it useful to search for internships that indicate that they accept applicants from your specific type of graduate program (e.g., school psychology).
   - If you are looking for half-time, 2-year internships, use the "Position Type > Part Time Funded" search option to locate such programs. Keep in mind that the number of available half-time internship positions tends to be very limited.

- You can search for any of the 60 "Training Opportunities" listed. For example, you could search for all programs that serve a Spanish-speaking population, conduct cognitive rehabilitation, or specialize in child neuropsychology.
- You will find that each program's listing includes directions on how to obtain additional information about the program and its application requirements (most programs have either a website or a printed brochure available).
- You can use the "bookmark" feature in your web browser to save any search result for future reference.

In addition to the *APPIC Directory Online*, faculty members and fellow graduate students are often excellent sources of information about internships. Contacting students from your program who are currently on internship or who have recently completed an internship may allow you to benefit from their internship search experiences. In addition, faculty will often know of internship programs that have had positive experiences with other students from your program and thus may be particularly welcoming of your application.

For students who are looking for internships in California, the California Psychology Internship Council (see http://www.capic.net) publishes a directory of internship programs in that state. Most of these programs are neither APA accredited nor members of APPIC, and most do not participate in the APPIC Match. Many are unpaid experiences. In addition, these positions are generally limited to students who attend certain doctoral programs in California.

1c. *Subscribe to the Match-News E-mail List.* This list provides news, tips, and information directly from APPIC about the selection process and the Match. We strongly recommend that you subscribe to Match-News very early in the process, as the information provided can be very helpful. Match-News is a low-volume list, usually sending no more than five messages per month, and thus you will not be inundated with e-mail.

Step 2. Get More Information About Each Site

Once you have reviewed the information in the *APPIC Directory Online*, you should obtain as much information as possible about the sites in which you are interested. Most sites now have their internship information available on their websites, but a few still require you to send them a brief e-mail to request their printed materials (typically sent to you as a Word or PDF document). Review each site's materials to determine whether you are a good fit for their training program. This can sometimes be difficult, as many sites sound quite similar in their written materials. It may be helpful to review each site with your specific goals in mind (see Chapter 3 for a discussion on constructing goals for internship training).

As you review the materials for each site of interest, it may be helpful to record some specific information for each site. The "sample summary sheet" in Exhibit 1.2 is one example of how you might track and organize that information. In particular, we advise the following:

- Make a note of the application deadline for each site in which you are interested. Application deadlines vary and are easily missed if you are not careful.

Exhibit 1.2. *Sample Summary Sheet of Application Site Requirements*

Name of site:
Application deadline:
Site-specific application requirements:
Specific programs or rotations of interest:
Strengths of this program:
Weaknesses of this program:
Quality of fit:
Ideas about areas to highlight in cover letter:
Questions to ask:
Overall interest: 1   2   3   4   5
Notes:

- Make a note of any special eligibility or application requirements.
- Make notes about the aspects of each program that excite you and/or for which you are a particularly good fit (based on your background, interests, and experiences). You should also note any aspects of the programs that are negatives or a poor fit for what you are seeking, or areas in which you have questions or need more information. Recording your impressions at this stage will make it much easier for you to make decisions about where to apply and will also help you write a compelling cover letter for each program when you get to that stage of the process.

Step 3. Decide Where to Apply

Once you have gathered and reviewed the information about each program, you will need to make some decisions about where you wish to apply. Below are some suggestions.

- Carefully review the summary sheets that you created and rate your level of interest in each site. You may note that a site that initially appeared quite exciting became less so as you reviewed other sites, or vice versa.
- Review your site interests and preferences with your mentor or a trusted faculty member for his or her input and impressions. You may also wish to consult with your director of clinical training and/or students from your program who are currently attending or have recently completed internship. Such conversations may have an impact on your level of interest in some sites.
- Order the summary sheets from highest to lowest interest. Use this organizational mechanism to determine the sites to which you will apply. Limit your choices to no more than 15 sites.
- Begin gathering and organizing all the information that you will need (e.g., clinical hours, testing experience) to report on your applications (see Chapter 2, this volume, for more information on the AAPI Online).
- Begin collecting the materials necessary to complete your CV (e.g., dates of training, clinical supervisors' names and titles, authors for presentations or publications).
- Order one official copy of your transcript from each school or university at which you completed graduate-level work (regardless of whether you received a

graduate degree), sent by each school directly to the AAPI Online service. You should not order or send undergraduate transcripts. Please refer to the instructions within the AAPI Online service for detailed instructions and to obtain the form(s) that you will need to accompany your submitted transcripts.

- Identify three people whom you would like to ask to write your recommendation letters. Three letters are usually required by each site, and it's generally best not to send more letters than what is requested by each site.
- Make appointments and talk with these three potential references, asking directly about whether they would feel comfortable writing you strong letters of recommendation in support of your internship search.
- Provide each reference with a copy of your CV, goals for internship, a summary of your strengths and areas to highlight, and other important information that will make their letter writing as easy as possible. Do not wait until the last minute to do this, and do not do this too far in advance—prevent a rush job or a forgotten job.

Step 4. Develop a Helpful Mind-Set

As we have informally talked with, advised, and consoled students preparing for internship, four applicant mind-sets have consistently emerged as common psychological approaches to the internship process. Some people may consider these as stress-management strategies, coping processes, defense mechanisms, heuristics, unconscious slips, or socially constructed narratives. Whatever you choose to call them, you will undoubtedly identify with some of these cognitions and perhaps even notice them in your peers.

The following taxonomy of themes seems to capture the beliefs of most students preparing to apply for internship. As you review them, see whether your thinking matches any of these common beliefs and, if so, whether you are comfortable with your approach or whether it might be helpful to make some cognitive shifts.

The "Just do it!" mind-set. This mind-set is characterized by one or more of the following thoughts and beliefs:

- "Internship is just another hoop that I have to jump through to get my degree and get on with my life."
- "Internship isn't that important in the grand scheme of things, anyway."
- "I'll just do it and get it over with in the most painless way possible."
- "I'll take anything, anywhere, whatever I can get—because I can endure anything for one year."

The "I'm too prepared and talented for them" mind-set. This approach is characterized by one or more of the following thoughts and beliefs:

- "My practicum experiences were outstanding—probably the best in the country; I deserve to be a psychologist *now*; I don't want or need to do an internship."
- "My program was so fabulous; there couldn't possibly be anything else an internship site can teach me."

- "This is one of those easy sites; this year will be a breeze."
- "I'm smarter than most of the internship faculty at this site!"

The "This decision will determine my life course" mind-set. This mind-set is characterized by one or more of the following thoughts and beliefs:

- "Selecting an internship site is one of the most important decisions I'll ever make in my life."
- "My internship will either open up endless possibilities for my career or stifle my career forever."

The "I acknowledge reciprocity" mind-set. This approach is characterized by the following thought and belief:

- "This internship will present me with opportunities to enhance and refine my skills, and I have some talents and ideas that will benefit the site."

How does your current mind-set compare with the beliefs presented here? If you most closely identify with the first three mind-sets, you probably need an intervention . . . and fast! If your thoughts most closely match the reciprocity mind-set, you are on the right track (even if you struggle with some of the others some of the time), and you are likely to become more actualized as you learn more about the process. Clearly, the most grounded and useful stance to take is one that recognizes the interdependence between the intern and the trainers. The promotion of mutuality creates an atmosphere of respect, curiosity, and shared inquiry. It is important for you to realize that not only are you academically prepared to contribute in meaningful ways and expand your knowledge, you also bring your unique life experiences, personality, and perspectives to the training program. This is highly valued by sites and supervisors. In addition, you will have some wonderful opportunities to be exposed to new people, along with new ways of thinking and doing things that will enhance your skills as an emerging practitioner. In the end, regardless of how you classify your thoughts, the information that follows in this book will help you become better prepared, more poised, and well positioned. We hope that you will be able to present yourself as you intend.

THE NEXT STEP   Now that you have a grasp on the overarching tasks that you will need to accomplish in the internship application process, it is time to turn your attention to the actual application. In Chapter 2, we present the elements of the application and provide some suggestions and overarching principles for completing the process.

2   COMPLETING THE APPIC APPLICATION FOR PSYCHOLOGY INTERNSHIPS

After glancing over the long Association of Psychology Postdoctoral and Internship Centers (APPIC) Application for Psychology Internships (AAPI), you may see the job of completing the application as daunting. Keeping track of all your clinical tasks, such as counting and recording each hour of therapy, supervision, group work, assessment, test interpretation, and consultation, while recording the age, ethnicity, and diversity status of your clients, can be overwhelming. But it need not be if you break the tasks of gathering information and completing the AAPI into manageable pieces.

This chapter can help you do exactly that. It offers practical guidance and suggestions for completing the application and walks you through a simple example of how to translate clinical hours to the AAPI. This chapter helps you take a detailed inventory of your clinical skills and experiences. However, bear in mind that there is no single correct method for calculating and recording your hours. Several overarching principles are offered to guide you through completing the AAPI in a way that fairly and accurately represents your training history. The chapter includes a few samples of tables and worksheets that can be modified to suit your needs for organizing and tallying your own clinical hours and related experiences. (Many programs provide students with similar worksheets at the beginning of practicum, and the "Training Resources" section of the APPIC website includes practicum hours tracking spreadsheets that you may find useful.)

WHAT IS THE APPIC APPLICATION FOR PSYCHOLOGY INTERNSHIPS?

Many years ago, before a standard application form was developed, each internship program developed its own unique application form. The style of the applications had considerable variability in the format for recording hours and experiences and in the manner in which essay questions were posed. Thus, applicants had to devote a tremendous amount of time to completing many lengthy application forms.

http://dx.doi.org/10.1037/0000102-002
Internships in Psychology: The APAGS Workbook for Writing Successful Applications and Finding the Right Fit, Fourth Edition, by C. Williams-Nickelson, M. J. Prinstein, and W. G. Keilin

In the late 1990s, the AAPI was created by APPIC to make the process more efficient for applicants, to reduce applicant stress, and to create some standardization in the information sought by APPIC-member internship programs. At that time, the AAPI was provided as a template that students would download via the Internet and complete using a word processing program. Although this standardized application resulted in a huge saving of time for applicants, it still meant that applicants had to print each application form, gather the associated materials on paper (i.e., cover letter, letters of recommendation, transcripts), and mail this large packet to each internship site.

In 2009, APPIC took the next step and introduced an online version of the AAPI, called the "AAPI Online" service. This new service enabled students to create and submit their applications and all supporting materials directly to internship sites via the Internet, and individuals who provided letters of recommendation could upload those letters directly into the service. Furthermore, applicants submitted only one copy of their official graduate transcripts to the AAPI Online service. Although the AAPI Online does require applicants to pay a fee for each submitted application, it does provide substantial cost savings in not having to print and mail applications or obtain multiple copies of official transcripts.

The AAPI Online is updated and revised annually. Although the changes usually aren't major, the effort is ongoing to better meet the needs of applicants and to provide the information that internship programs find most important and helpful. It is very important to review the AAPI Online as soon as it becomes available (usually in July) so that you have time to gather the necessary data to complete it.

Keep in mind that although the AAPI is very important, it is only one of a series of items and information that will be used to evaluate your potential to succeed and your fit with a particular site. Keeping the internship tasks in perspective throughout the application process can help you maintain a grounded mind-set.

AAPI ONLINE OVERVIEW

The AAPI Online consists for four separate "portals"—in other words, four ways to access the service depending upon one's role in the process:

- The "Applicant Portal": Used by applicants to access the AAPI Online service and to create and submit their applications
- The "DCT Portal": Used by directors of clinical training (DCTs) to verify their students' hours and provide evaluative feedback
- The "Reference Portal": Used by faculty, past supervisors, or others who may be submitting reference information in support of students' applications
- The "Selection Portal": Used by internship training directors to access applications that have been submitted by students

APPIC requires that all applications be submitted electronically via the AAPI Online service and that a site may not request a printed copy of your application. Keep in mind that each internship site has its own application requirements and deadlines, and it is very important to have a system to keep track of these requirements so that your submitted applications can be timely and accurate.

The AAPI Online has a comprehensive set of instructions embedded within the service that will answer many of your questions. You may access the full set of instructions by clicking on the "Instructions" link within the "Help" section on the left side of each page or on the "Instructions for this section" link at the top of each data entry page.

Here is a step-by-step guide to navigating the AAPI Online service:

1. *Create an Account:* You can access the AAPI Online from the APPIC website (http://www.appic.org); click on the "AAPI/APPA" pull-down menu. There is no charge to create an account. In fact, if you wish to create a test account to try out the service before creating your real account, you are welcome to do so.

2. *Submit Graduate Transcripts:* We recommend starting this process as early as possible so that any delays don't affect your ability to submit applications. You are required to submit *official* copies of *all* graduate transcripts to the AAPI Online service, regardless of whether you received a degree. Do not submit any undergraduate transcripts. If you completed both undergraduate and graduate training at the same institution, your undergraduate record will likely be included on your transcript along with your graduate work, but this won't be a problem. After logging into your AAPI Online account, you should print a "Transcript Request Form" and provide it to the transcript office for each institution, with the instructions to include that form with your official transcripts. Once this process is complete, AAPI Online will automatically attach a copy of your transcripts to each application that you submit.

3. *Request References:* Beginning in 2015, APPIC required reference information to be submitted on a form called the APPIC Standardized Reference Form. This form was developed to ensure that those who provide references will address predefined areas of applicants' professional functioning. The Standardized Reference Form is a Microsoft Word document that is downloaded and completed by each individual who is providing a reference and is then uploaded directly by the reference-writer into the AAPI Online.

   Once you have decided who will be providing your references, you should send each of them an electronic request through the AAPI Online service. This generates an e-mailed request to each reference and provides them with instructions about how to upload their completed Standardized Reference Form. You will receive a notification whenever this form is uploaded on your behalf. Since references are considered confidential, you will not be permitted to view them (although a reference-writer may choose to give you a copy if they wish to do so).

   Most sites ask for three recommendations, and most applicants send the same three to all sites to which they are applying. However, it is acceptable to (a) ask for more than three people to serve as references to send different letters to different sites and/or (b) have a single reference write multiple versions of his or her letter. You should be judicious about using either of these options and do so only when sending different versions of letters to different sites is necessary (e.g., if you are applying to very different settings or types of sites that might call for different things to be emphasized in each letter). Consult with your advisor and/or references if you aren't sure of the best approach.

4. *Develop Your Application:* This involves going through the various sections of the AAPI Online and providing information about your education and training experiences. Be sure to allow sufficient time for this step, as it can be time-consuming—and even more so if your records of your graduate experiences

are incomplete. In addition, you will need to develop your cover letters, essay responses, and curriculum vitae (CV). Some sites may request supplemental material, which is an item that is required by a specific site but is not a part of the standard AAPI. The only permitted supplemental materials are a treatment/case summary and/or a psychological evaluation report. If a site requests you to submit something else (e.g., your undergraduate transcripts, an additional essay response, a special form), that request may be a violation of APPIC policies, and you should contact the AAPI Online coordinator for guidance.

5. *Submit to DCT for Verification:* Once you have completed entering your practicum experiences, you must submit this information to your DCT for review and verification. The information is locked upon submission to your DCT, which means that you can no longer make any changes. Thus, be sure you have carefully reviewed the accuracy of your information before submission. In addition to verifying your hours, your DCT will answer some questions about your graduate training and internship readiness (e.g., whether the faculty considers you ready for internship) and provide a summary evaluation of your background, skills, and experiences. The evaluative information provided by your DCT is considered confidential, and thus, you are not permitted to view it. In the event that your DCT does not approve of your submission, he or she can return it to you, and it will then be temporarily unlocked for you to make the necessary changes.

6. *Select Your Designations:* The term *designation*, as used within the AAPI Online, simply means an internship site to which you are applying. For each site that you designate, you will identify the cover letter, references, essays, CV, and optional supplemental materials that you wish to be submitted along with the basic application. In the event that a site offers multiple rotations or "programs" (e.g., a neuropsychology rotation, an outpatient rotation), you must designate the program(s) to which you are applying.

7. *Submit Your Applications:* You may begin submitting your completed applications to sites in early October. Be careful not to miss any deadlines and that you follow any specific application instructions that may be included on sites' websites or brochures. For peace of mind, it is recommended that you submit each application no later than 48 hours before the application deadline, just in case technical problems or other issues interfere with the submission process. You are given the option to view a formatted version of your AAPI before submitting. You will be charged a fee for each submitted application, and the per application cost increases substantially if you submit more than 15 applications. Once submitted, your applications will be instantly delivered to each internship program.

The elements that make up a completed application with the AAPI Online are as follows (please note that more information about many of these elements is provided in later chapters of this workbook).

1. The basic or core part of your application, including contact information, educational background, current graduate program, professional conduct, and a summary of your practicum experience.

2. A cover letter. You are expected to submit a different cover letter to each site. Sending a generic cover letter to sites will not be viewed positively.
3. A CV. You may use the same CV for all sites to which you apply, or you may upload multiple versions and choose the version that is submitted to each site.
4. Responses to four essay questions. You may use the same essays for all sites or you may create multiple versions.
5. Verification of Internship Eligibility and Readiness (completed by your DCT as described above).
6. Standardized Reference Forms.
7. Supplemental materials.
8. Official copies of graduate transcripts.

The remainder of this chapter provides general information on completing the AAPI Online as well as information about how to record your practicum experiences. In Chapter 3 we provide detailed information about identifying your goals, writing cover letters, and answering the essay questions, and in Chapter 4 we discuss CVs, recommendation letters, and supplemental materials.

COMPLETING THE AAPI

What follows are general principles and tips—some *do*s and *don't*s—that will help you organize your approach to the AAPI.

- *Do* visit the APPIC website (http://www.appic.org) to review the general AAPI Online instructions along with the "Frequently Asked Questions" section.
- *Do* get in the habit of reading the instructions that are contained within each section of the AAPI Online service.
- *Don't* send each site the exact same cover letter. For each site to which you apply, it is *essential* that your cover letter addresses the unique aspects of the site that interest you, and that you discuss why your interests, background, and experiences are a great fit for that specific site.
- *Don't* assume that the person reviewing your application knows all about you and your program. Applicants often omit training details that they assume to be universal but actually are unique and important for the internship site to know.
- *Don't* tally all your hours from logs, calendars, or loose sheets of paper just before sitting down to complete the AAPI. Develop an organized record-keeping system with cumulative totals early in your training. You will need to know many details about the setting, age, gender, ethnicity, diversity status, and type of direct service provided at each practicum site. Start recording these details during your first practicum.
- *Do* organize and review your practicum log sheets for accuracy and clarity before completing the AAPI. A mathematical error early on can take hours to find down the road.
- *Don't* count all your learning experiences as bona fide practicum hours. For example, practicing the administration of a test on your partner or a classmate and participating in mock sessions as class demonstrations do not count as practicum hours.
- *Do* be honest in reporting your hours and experiences.

- *Don't* become obsessive or paranoid about ensuring that every fraction of an hour is reported accurately and reflected in the proper category!
- *Do* ask your DCT all your "Can I count . . .?" questions about reporting your practicum hours. Your DCT is ultimately responsible for verifying that your practicum hours are appropriate and supervised. You are responsible for knowing (and reporting) that practicum hours are those obtained: (a) by practicing your skills; (b) under appropriate supervision; (c) as part of an organized, sequential training experience; (d) with real clients; and (e) in real treatment settings.
- *Do* use your best judgment and realize that you will not be brought up on ethics charges if you make a benign mistake.
- *Don't* inflate your numbers or experiences to try to make you appear more compatible with a particular site.
- *Don't* misrepresent yourself.
- *Do* remember that you will have many blank spaces on your application when it comes to practicum hours and experiences. The AAPI Online has many categories, and it isn't possible for you or anyone else to have had most or all the experiences listed.
- *Do* read the AAPI instructions and follow them. Every attempt has been made to ensure that the instructions are clear, but if you become confused or have an unusual situation, consult with others to determine the best method for reporting your experience.
- *Don't* submit your AAPI without having it reviewed and edited by your peers and faculty.
- *Do* edit your AAPI on more than one occasion and over a period of time.
- *Do* use the "Save" feature frequently as you are completing the AAPI Online. In particular, don't navigate away from any page or section without first saving your work.
- *Do* ask individuals who will be providing letters of recommendation, "Can you write a letter of strong support?"
- *Don't* press someone to write a recommendation who articulates any reservations or shows any hesitancy to your request. Unusually vague or bad letters of recommendation can damage your chances of being matched to an internship.
- *Do* carefully consider the type of autobiographical information you provide in your essays. Pay attention to your reasons for sharing sensitive information, such as your ethnic heritage, age, relationship status, socioeconomic status, sexuality, family obligations, visible or invisible disability, and gender. Sometimes, sharing this information can increase your chances for being highly ranked because the program seeks and respects diversity and wants to know about who you are as a person. Other times, this information may be interpreted as indicative of loose boundaries or too much personal disclosure. The best approach is to share what you determine to be most congruent with who you are, what you want to convey about yourself, and what you value in your approach to clinical work and supervision.
- *Don't* write an autobiographical statement that suggests severe psychopathology. It may not be appropriate to share information about your own psychiatric hospitalizations or that you selected psychology as a career because you wanted to learn more about your own disorders!

- *Do* remember that this is an evaluative process, and sites are using this information not only to determine your clinical talent and fit with their training philosophy and opportunities but also to decide whether you are someone who is relatively healthy mentally and someone whom they will enjoy working with for a year or more.
- *Do* contact APPIC if you have difficulties with completing or submitting your applications or if you have questions that aren't answered in the instructions or by your DCT. APPIC has an AAPI Online coordinator who is available to address questions or hear your feedback about the AAPI Online; his or her name is listed in the "Contact" section of the APPIC website. If you are experiencing technical problems with the AAPI Online service, such as logging in or submitting applications or transcripts, you may contact the AAPI Online technical support team at support@appicas.org or (617) 612-2899 (calls are answered Monday through Friday from 9:00 am to 5:00 pm Eastern Standard Time).

SUMMARIZING YOUR PRACTICUM EXPERIENCES ON THE AAPI

The amount of time that it will take to summarize and record your practicum experiences on your application is directly related to the extent to which you accurately and comprehensively recorded your experiences throughout graduate school. We hope that your doctoral program gave you proper guidance in this regard from the moment you walked in their door. The last thing you want to have to do at this point is to try to remember the specifics of several years of practicum experiences.

Even if you have been meticulous about recording and counting your experiences along the way, summarizing and recording them on the AAPI can be both tedious and challenging. First, it is stressful because it triggers those long-standing worries about whether you have enough hours to be competitive. Second, how to transcribe your hours from your tracking system to the AAPI can be confusing, as you will soon discover that it isn't always obvious or clear as to how certain experiences should be categorized on the AAPI. Although the AAPI Online does provide some specific guidance, you will sometimes find that a particular training experience can legitimately be listed in any of several categories.

It is important to remember that there is often no right answer as to how a particular experience should be categorized, and you will need to use your best judgment. We suggest that you keep in mind the following principles when making your decisions.

- Be honest and reasonable.
- Consult the AAPI Online instructions for the relevant categories.
- Use your best judgment.
- If in doubt, consult with your DCT.
- If still in doubt, consult with the APPIC AAPI Online coordinator.

As a rule, consult your DCT if you have any questions about how to count or record your clinical experiences.

You are not expected to have experience in all, or even most, of the areas listed on the AAPI. A comprehensive list of possible clinical activities is provided so that applicants may easily complete the application, but this in no way implies that those are experiences that you are expected to have had. Be sure to keep this in mind as you notice that there are many categories that you will leave blank. Blanks do not imply a deficiency in your training or areas that you should immediately seek experience in; rather, they indicate that the particular training may not be relevant to you or the site, or they may show that you are trainable in certain areas, which some sites find appealing.

The five main categories in which you will record and summarize your practicum experiences are listed below.

1. Intervention Experience
2. Psychological Assessment Experience
3. Supervision Received
4. Additional Information About Practicum Experiences
5. Support Activities

Be sure to follow the AAPI instructions for further clarification about what constitutes a practicum hour and how to record these hours. In short, hours must

- have been accrued through November 1 (another section of the AAPI allows you to summarize and describe any anticipated practicum experiences that will occur after November 1 and prior to the beginning of your internship),
- have been a part of formal academic training/credit or sanctioned by your graduate program,
- have been supervised,
- be listed separately for those acquired as part of your master's degree training and those acquired as part of your doctoral training,
- be calculated by actual hours (although a 50-min session = 1 practicum hour), and
- be counted only once (i.e., the same hour cannot be recorded or counted in different categories, with the exception of the "Additional Information About Practicum Experiences" section). When you have an hour that falls under more than one area, select the one category that you feel best captures the experience. For example, a stress-management group may be counted as a group therapy hour or as a medical/health-related intervention, but not both.

The AAPI also asks for the number of different individuals, groups, families, and couples to whom you have provided services. For example, if you ran a group with 12 individuals in it for 10 weeks, you would record the number "1" in the "number of different groups" category.

Some graduate students may have excellent clinical experiences that were acquired as part of their work history or volunteer service activities. Because this type of experience is not program-sanctioned or supervised, it cannot be included with your practicum hours. However, the AAPI does include a section in which students may describe these other work-related or volunteer activities. Similarly, students also may describe their teaching experiences.

In the "Psychological Assessment Experience" section, you may list your experience with a variety of testing instruments. The AAPI provides a list of the more common assessment instruments, and you may add any others that you have used that are not included on that list. For each assessment instrument, you are asked to designate the number that you administered and scored, the number of reports that you wrote that included that measure, and the number that you administered as part of a research project.

A separate section for "Integrated Reports" allows you to indicate the number of comprehensive psychological reports that you wrote. Be sure to check the definition of "integrated report" as described in the AAPI Online instructions.

SUMMARY

Calculating your clinical hours and experiences is not usually a fun process; it can be frustrating and confusing even for the most organized individual. However, this task must be accomplished to complete the AAPI and to demonstrate to prospective sites that you have accumulated valuable experiences that make you a good fit for their training opportunities. It is important to start the process of organizing and recording your hours as soon as you begin your practicum. Good documentation will help you easily and swiftly transfer your direct service hours, testing/assessment experience, and client demographic information to the AAPI. If you have questions about the types of hours that you may count or where to include certain hours on your AAPI, you should always consult your DCT. Remember, there are no absolute answers regarding how you count and record your clinical experiences. Because of this, working closely with your DCT and simply using your best judgment are critical.

After recording your hours, you are ready to begin thinking about your internship and career goals and how to clearly articulate them in your essays. You now have a good sense of where your training gaps exist and what clinical areas are of interest to you. In the next chapter, we walk you through the process of identifying goals and writing essays that reflect who you are and the best type of training environment for your internship year.

3

GOALS, ESSAYS, AND THE COVER LETTER

SETTING
GOALS

Many students embarking on the internship application process have established a clear and determined goal: to get a match. This indeed is an important goal, but it is perhaps not entirely sufficient to help you successfully find a training experience that will allow you to fulfill your dreams as a psychologist. In this chapter, we briefly discuss the importance of setting training goals and the manner in which doing so will help you to craft exceptional essays. We also discuss each essay in detail and provide examples and suggestions for mastering this part of the process.

Remember many years ago when you thought it would be fun and interesting to earn a doctoral degree in clinical, counseling, or school psychology? At that time, you may have had some ideas about what you wanted to do professionally after graduation. Perhaps you dreamt of starting a private practice or working in a medical setting, a counseling center, or a secondary school or as a professor in academia. If you are like most graduate students, you probably have spent the last 3 to 6 years or more working on very specific deadlines for classes, clients, theses, and comprehensive exams, and it has been somewhat difficult to take a step back and think about what the ultimate goal of training would be. In fact, many graduate students are more confused about their career goals at this late stage in training than they were when they were first accepted for doctoral study!

Fear not! You will have a career, and it will be worth all your training! But first, you need to make sure that you have charted a course that will help you to be best prepared for whatever career path you choose. This is why, before you dive into essay writing, it is absolutely essential that you develop a clear set of training goals for internship. Doing so will help make this process transcend being just another training "hoop" that you must accomplish and instead become a time of introspection, professional growth, and maturity as an independent psychologist. Once you have a clear sense of your goals,

---

http://dx.doi.org/10.1037/0000102-003

Internships in Psychology: The APAGS Workbook for Writing Successful Applications and Finding the Right Fit, Fourth Edition, by C. Williams-Nickelson, M. J. Prinstein, and W. G. Keilin

you also will be surprised by how much easier it is to write your essays and to respond to interview questions later in this process. In short, goals are the ingredient that separates the more focused, mature, thoughtful, and deliberate applicant from the others, and they are the ingredient that can help to ensure that your internship experience is the best possible fit for you.

GOALS, ESSAYS, AND THE COVER LETTER

Setting goals is a collaborative process that results from discussion with your advisor, clinical supervisors, other students, and perhaps your training director. You may want to schedule some meetings to have frank discussions about your own strengths and weaknesses, as well as the strengths and weaknesses of your training program. Take careful notes of these discussions, and think about your own experiences of when you felt most or least comfortable during your training. You soon will have to make a decision to be in a particular type of setting for a full year, engaging in some very specific clinical and training activities. It will be important that such an experience will help you to feel competent and happy and will contribute to your growth as a psychologist-in-training.

It also will be important to think quite seriously about potential long-term plans for your career. This is perhaps the most difficult part of the process. Once you have finished your interviews, you will have been exposed to a variety of settings in which psychologists practice and to multiple models of careers in psychology. This exposure usually assists in achieving greater clarity of long-term career options. But at this stage of the application process, it may be better to think more about careers that you would rule out rather than those you would rule in. It is likely that you already know that there are some activities (e.g., therapy, assessment, research, teaching) that you most certainly will want to engage in during your career in large proportion and other activities that you would prefer to minimize. Next, think about what expertise will help you most in achieving such a career. For example, students who wish to enter private practice should be very comfortable with efficacious treatment for the most common presentations of psychopathology in an outpatient setting (e.g., for adults: depression, anxiety, Axis II disorders; for youth: attention-deficit/hyperactivity disorder and oppositional defiant disorder). Students who wish to teach may want to obtain broad exposure to severe psychopathology to assist them in developing lectures on the breadth of psychological symptoms. Students who wish to work in a medical setting likely will want exposure to such an environment and will want to participate on multidisciplinary teams of health care professionals. You will likely want to develop specific areas of your expertise as a specialty (e.g., modalities of treatment, diagnoses, assessment of treatment techniques), and thus you may wish to seek focused, intensive training experiences in these areas.

Consider that your internship may be the last focused, intensive training experience in your career. Some students will obtain a postdoctoral fellowship after internship; however, in many cases this experience will be highly specialized. Thus, your internship truly is an opportunity to get broad exposure and intensive training as a student. In short, it will be important to consider the following when you are looking into internships.

1. Given my accrued experiences and areas of emerging competency to date, what are the most essential experiences that I need to obtain to become a _____ (insert range of potential career objectives here)?

2. By the time I am a licensed, independent psychologist, I would like to feel that I am competent and autonomous in_____ (insert specific skill/ knowledge domain here).
3. I could probably function somewhat independently in a few areas right now, but I feel that I should get more experience doing_____ (insert specific activity here) before I could feel confident as a psychologist.

It may be helpful to use the worksheet in Exhibit 3.1 to organize your thoughts about your goals.

Exhibit 3.1. *Goals Worksheet*

It is important for you to be able to clearly articulate your short- and long-term training and career goals. To do this, you should begin to take inventory now. It is always good to write your ideas down on paper so that you can revisit and revise them regularly.

1. I have a lot of experience in:

2. I am lacking experience in:

3. My supervisors suggest that I should learn more about:

4. Do I want a generalist or specialty experience on internship? Why? My goals for internship are:

   1.

   2.

   3.

   My short-term career goals are:

   1.

   2.

   3.

   My longer term career goals are:

   1.

   2.

   3.

It is hoped that by the time you are done with this process, you will have generated two to four specific training goals for internship. These goals may be somewhat precise, referring to specific experiences, populations, modalities, or activities that you desire for internship training. It is important that you feel that you could justify each one of these goals (i.e., explain why you have selected this training goal in particular), and these training goals should distinguish you as a unique applicant.

(continues)

Exhibit 3.1. *(Continued)*

The following are examples of specific training goals that may help prompt the development of your own goals:

1. I would like to get more experience with behavioral treatments for attention-deficit/hyperactivity disorder.
2. I would like more exposure to severe psychopathology, including psychopathy, in a forensic setting.
3. I would like more experience conducting family therapy (or group therapy, or assessments to diagnose a specific disorder, etc.).
4. I would like to conduct research while on internship and to be exposed to scientist–practitioner careers.
5. I would like to learn more about the counseling center environment and develop expertise with young adults' difficulties.
6. I would like to establish a career and professional network in the Anchorage area.
7. I would like to go to a site that will allow for postdoctoral training.

The following are examples of less specific goals that, by themselves, do not successfully differentiate applicants because they are too vague and lack depth and evidence of introspection:

1. I would like to conduct outpatient treatment with adults.
2. I would like to attend a prestigious site.
3. I would like to become a competent psychologist in the area of assessment.
4. I hope to enjoy my experience on internship by working in many different areas.
5. I am excited about internship and see a large range of possibilities at your site.

GUIDELINES FOR WRITING ESSAYS

Now that you have your goals, you are ready to write your essays! The composition of brief essays does not seem as if it would take a long time, and yet it most certainly does. You may (and should) go through many drafts, and you should solicit feedback from many sources. After several drafts, you may find it difficult to read your own work objectively or to retain the ability to scrutinize your work as carefully as you might review an unfamiliar piece of writing. For these reasons, it is very important to allow ample time to construct your essays. This is the only piece of the application process that is still under your control. You already have accrued your practicum experiences, and your letter writers already have formed impressions of your skills. These essays are an excellent opportunity for you to help the reader of your application understand the story and the person that is "between the lines" of your curriculum vitae (CV) and the objective Association of Psychology Postdoctoral and Internship Centers (APPIC) Application for Psychology Internships (AAPI) information. It is worth substantial effort to ensure that your essays convey your experiences, ideas, reflections, and personality in an accurate and compelling way. This will take some time.

One reason the essays may be so difficult to write is that they require a different writing style from the type of writing that was required of you during graduate training (i.e., for theses and clinical reports). This writing is in the first person, and you very much want your voice to be prominent in the text. This is not to say that you should write informally or use slang, but it also is not necessary for you to demonstrate your high Graduate Record Examinations verbal score with the pretentious use of fancy vocabulary. Be yourself, assuming that you indeed are an intelligent, educated, conscientious student who is about to become a learned professional in society.

It is extremely important to remember that your essays will be read by members of admissions committees who have read dozens of others' essays in the same sitting. Thus, clarity is paramount. Short, pithy sentences with simple ideas often work best. You will have spent hours crafting these documents; the ideas within them need to be extremely clear to a reader who will spend a mere minute or two on each one. Few will go back to reread confusing sentences, and even fewer will shuffle between your essays to capture the continuity of your ideas or implicit, subtle themes. You must be explicit in what you are attempting to convey, and you should expect to be repetitive in your main messages.

Your essays should accomplish several objectives. First, you want to offer a genuine reflection of your aspirations for internship training. Honesty is essential to ensure that you not only get a match but that you also get matched to a site that is best for you. Getting matched to a site that is a poor fit for you will lead to a very unhappy year that will compromise your training experiences and undermine your confidence and competence. Do not write essays that say what you believe the training committee wants to hear. Trust that there is a match for you—the real you. Second, it is important to present yourself as a unique psychologist-in-training. Read each paragraph of your essay draft, and ask yourself, "Have I written anything in this section that couldn't also have been written by 75% of other applicants to this site?" If the answer is no, then you need some more "you" in that essay. Naturally, you do not want to differentiate yourself using a gimmick (a silly anecdote, story, or peculiar "oversharing"), but you do want to ensure that your ideas reflect the unique person you are, given your unique training path to date.

It may be helpful to approach the essays with the following ideas in mind. For the past several years, you have been identified mostly as a student in a specific program as mentored by a specific advisor. You likely have introduced yourself to psychologists in the field with this information as markers of your professional identity. Your experiences in the field largely have been contained within the walls of your psychology department at your university.

This application process requires you to establish and convey a more specific identity that is unique to you. You are still the product of your program and advisor's mentorship, but this no longer is sufficient to describe the psychologist-in-training that you are now and the psychologist that you hope to be. Your path to doctoral study was unique; your reasons for attending your program and the choices you have made while engaged in it are part of your individual story. More important, the constellation of experiences you have accrued and the reflections you have had on these experiences throughout graduate school are unique to you and you alone. Why did you choose these specific practicum placements, and why did you select your specific thesis topics? What were your reactions to each of these experiences, and how did these reactions help shape your opinions about current issues in the field? What are your unique training goals, and how did you develop them? This is your story, and this is what you want to reflect in your essays (and interviews). This story differs from every other applicant's, and this is what makes you a unique candidate for a specific site.

You have 2,000 words with which to accomplish these objectives, divided among one very important cover letter and four specific essays. The story is a continuous one that starts with an "abstract" to your application that reviews the major themes and areas of fit (the cover letter), followed by a description of your experiences and goals (Essay 1); elaborates through a discussion of your thoughts on a few important issues in our field today (e.g., theoretical conceptualization/orientation, client diversity) in Essays 2 and 3; and then focuses on your specific research interests in Essay 4.

A discussion of each specific essay is included below, followed by a discussion of the cover letter. We discuss the cover letter last because students typically work on this document after they have finished their initial four essays. We also have included some examples of actual essays used by applicants in recent years (with identifying information modified). With these applicants' permission, we have included, first, one example of a first draft, comments, and the corresponding final draft of an Essay 1, with additional final draft samples, to help you see the evolution of the writing process. The chapter then discusses and provides examples of final drafts of Essays 2 through 4, as well as a sample cover letter.

Note that the online AAPI will allow you to write several different versions of your essays, and then append the appropriate versions to each specific application. For Essays 1 through 4, you may not need to construct different versions if you have been consistent in your internship goals. However, if you find that you are applying to quite different types of sites (e.g., counseling centers vs. Veterans Affairs settings), then you may indeed want to craft modified versions of your essays for each type of site and be sure to upload the appropriate version for each different type of site.

AUTOBIOGRAPHICAL STATEMENT, ESSAY 1

Please provide an autobiographical statement. (There is no "correct" format for this question.) Answer this question as if someone had asked you, "Tell me something about yourself." It is an opportunity for you to provide the internship site with some information about yourself. It is entirely up to you to decide what information you wish to provide along with the format in which to present it.

Essay 1 often is considered the most difficult essay because it also has the most ambiguous purpose. It is also not possible to write a full autobiography in 500 words, unless you seriously lack depth. Some sites prefer to get to know you as a person, including interests both inside and outside of psychology. The committee may wish to obtain some insight regarding your personality and background and perhaps catch a glimpse of the kind of person you would be during a social interaction. Other sites might be most interested in a professional autobiography, including a discussion of the factors that led to your decision to pursue a career in psychology and a brief review of your experiences, culminating in a discussion of your goals for internship training. Still other sites are interested in assessing how you decided to approach this essay, having no preconceived opinion of a type of essay that is preferable.

How do you know what the site wants to hear? It is unfortunate, but you will not know. Some anecdotal evidence suggests that many counseling centers or sites with psychodynamic training may prefer the personal approach, whereas research-oriented sites or sites with a cognitive behavioral orientation might prefer a focus on your professional history. Ultimately, this is a decision that you will need to make on the basis of your own comfort level and disposition. Remember, you are not merely looking for a slot; you are looking for a good fit. If the autobiographical statement truly reflects your style, you increase the chances that you will find a true fit.

Still, this is a hard task. The following tips will help you get started with the autobiographical statement.

- *Tell a story.* In other words, describe yourself and your experience in a manner that has a beginning, a middle, and an end. You may wish to start with a depiction of the person you were before graduate school and end with the person you want to be after internship. You may also want to select one story out of your autobiography to highlight that has been particularly meaningful to you in your development as a psychologist.

- *State your goals.* Explain to the reader where your internship goals came from. Demonstrate to the committee that these are well-thought-out goals that were developed through a careful review of your past experiences and career objectives. You may even wish to discuss these goals with a supervisor for assistance. If your goals seem to be tacked on to the end of the essay with no explanation or foreshadowing, a cynical reviewer may think that you have disingenuously changed them for each site to "appear" to be a match.

- *Do not restate your CV.* Rather, walk the reader through it. What are the most important experiences on your CV? What are the themes that have emerged across all your experiences? Is there something you are especially proud of that you would like to highlight? Don't talk about what you did but, rather, what you thought while doing it.

- *Talk about the future.* Internship sites know what they are good at and where their interns have gone following training. Giving them a sense of where you may want to go will help the committee to know whether they can provide you with the experiences you need. Although you may not need to have a clear idea of your future plans (most do not at this stage), you can probably rule in or out at least two or three options.

Recall that Essay 1, if structured properly, could serve as an organizing theme for the entire set of essays. Hence, you should embed statements about your approach to cases, your experience with diversity, your research goals, and your fit with the site. By constructing the first essay in this manner, your set of essays is more likely to read as a detailed description of you as a professional rather than as a series of fragmented details.

How do you do that? It will probably take several drafts—at least one or two that help you to learn about yourself, and then a few more that involve polish to get it ready for submission. On those first few drafts, we have found that an especially helpful approach is to reframe the task to make it far less daunting and confusing. Below, we explain how.

Imagine you were writing a letter to a friend (rather than an essay—as the notion of which may induce writer's block). Imagine that friend wants to know what you hope to learn on internship. But before you simply list your three goals, you need to explain why and how you got to these goals. Start by mentioning a little bit about the person you were before you applied to graduate school. This may involve some recollections about your upbringing, or perhaps some educational experience in high school or college. Whatever it is, consider sharing that information specifically to help explain why you reacted to your graduate school educational experiences the way you did. For instance, perhaps you were a track star in college, and it has made you especially oriented toward tenacity and endurance. Maybe you considered being an architect, and you now approach all your cases in a very structured, piecewise way. Perhaps you come from a large family, and you have since been fascinated by interpersonal perspectives. Whatever it is—explore what makes you the kind of psychologist you have become and try and do so in a brief intro to your essay about your life before graduate school. Keep this part brief—no more than about 150 words. This approximate word limit is important—if your essay is dominated by a discussion of what led you to graduate school, then you are spending too much time talking about what you share with most applicants (i.e., being interested in the field and getting into a doctoral program) than you are what makes you unique (i.e., your graduate training).

Once you have talked a bit about your unique path, discuss your experiences in graduate school, particularly the clinical experiences. Remember that you don't need to discuss them chronologically, or exhaustively. Nor do you need to comment on all them with equal space. Simply mention the ones that motivated you towards your internship goals. For instance, you might mention that your family therapy practicum made you discover you prefer individual therapy or that an assessment rotation inspired you to get more experience with severe populations. Note that this discussion is not meant to restate your CV but to review your experiences—and most important, your reactions to each of these experiences—to help explain why you selected your specific internship goals.

Once you have done so, you will likely want to restate those goals at the end of the essay and help tie it all together for the reader. Note that it is essential that you have addressed all these goals within the body of the essay before you state them at the end. If your goals read like a surprise ending, or an unjustified objective, it may seem like an insincere addition to the essay that you listed in a desperate attempt to match!

Below is an example of a first draft of an autobiographical statement, followed by comments that are common for many students as they write this statement.

Essay 1, First Draft

I did not always want to be a psychologist. Actually, it was not until the second semester of my junior year that I found the profession. There was not some big incident or exciting story behind my changing from economics to psychology. In fact, my professional identity has continued to slowly evolve from that initial switch, and now, I could not imagine another career that would be better suited to me. Every step in the evolution has added an important perspective or life goal, and I feel fortunate to have been able to pursue this path.

The allure of working with children first drew my attention to psychology as a career. Working as a child clinician resonated with my sense of fun and imagination. When I started doing clinical work with children, I also loved having to always think on my feet and being drawn into their worlds. I found it challenging to think about how to help a 7-year-old change his or her behavior, thoughts, or feelings but also about how different it would be to help a 15-year-old. I take pleasure in knowing that every time I walk into a room with kids, anything can happen. In my clinical work, I also find inspiration for research and how to examine psychopathology. Moreover, the aspects of my personality that fit child clinical work (sense of fun, curiosity, energetic, and imagination) also help me be a better researcher and teacher.

Although I had participated in research at college, it was not until I developed my own research questions and tested them that I began to see research as a part of my professional identity. I became involved in an applied developmental research laboratory working with Latino immigrants. Taking part in both design and data collection of an intervention study, I began to see how clinical work and research both inform one another. At this time, my own research questions began to surface, and as I watched parents, children, and teachers interacting, I became interested in the interpersonal aspects of maladaptive behavior.

Teaching was the last aspect of the profession to which I was exposed, but one that I find immensely satisfying. Since starting graduate school, I have taught my own course, mentored students on their own research projects, and supervised students doing clinical work. In all these teaching endeavors, I have hoped to instill an appreciation for curiosity, passion, knowledge, and cultural differences. Moreover, like my clinical work, teaching also provides me with continued energy for my own research.

My current professional path is as a matter of fact not that different from my initial career goal. By first grade, I wanted to become a doctor and join the Peace Corps so that I could provide medical services to those with no access. What drew me to that profession at such a young age is probably what drives my current professional goals to become a clinical psychology professor researching clinical interventions in underserved populations, specifically Latinos. My compassion and dedication to helping the underserved have not wavered, and I do not need to go to a developing nation. Fewer than 1% of psychologists are Latinos, and as a professor I will be able to be a model for other minority students, challenge and teach undergraduates to be cognizant of cultural issues, and train future clinicians in cultural competence. At each step of my path, whether it be clinical work, research, or teaching, I have increased my skills and knowledge. I look forward to continue evolving on internship, where I hope to get added training.

Essay 1, Comments

This is a well-written essay that effectively achieves several of the objectives outlined above. Indeed, as a first draft, this student has done a terrific job in many respects. First, the essay tells a compelling story with a beginning, middle, and end. It is clear how this student's interests have evolved over time, and a clear set of career goals has been articulated. Second, the essay is written in a knowledgeable yet personal voice.

This essay could be improved in several ways. First, although the story of the applicant's decision to enter graduate school is compelling and interesting, the text regarding the decision to enter doctoral studies dominates about two thirds of the essay. This is common among first drafts; they often sound a lot like the essay that was used when applying to graduate school, rather than an essay that is focused on internship. Given that all applicants at this stage have already made the decision to pursue a graduate career, and all have already been in graduate training, this information is not as useful in helping to describe what kind of psychologist-in-training the applicant is now. It may be more helpful to discuss the graduate experiences that have shaped this applicant's internship goals.

It is also common, in autobiographical essay first drafts, for internship goals not to have been clearly articulated. Rather, the strongest message that is conveyed in this draft is that the applicant is enthusiastic about clinical child psychology. This is a wonderful sentiment to convey; however, it may not adequately distinguish the applicant from others. From the perspective of an internship selection committee, it is difficult to determine whether this student will thrive at a specific site and whether the site is a good fit. It would be helpful to understand what kind of psychologist-in-training this applicant has become and what principles guide this applicant's decisions.

Last, this essay is overly modest. This applicant has achieved a great deal while in graduate school, but those achievements have not been adequately reflected in the essay.

Essay 1, Final Draft

Clinical work first drew me into the profession of psychology. When I started doing clinical work with children, I enjoyed the challenge of helping children understand their emotional worlds and change through the use of cognitive behavioral techniques. Yet, I realized that integrating other theoretical perspectives, such as developmental approaches, significantly improved therapeutic responses. Nevertheless, because the majority of interventions did not address issues of diversity, I found myself having to adapt treatments to fit the cultural contexts of my clients. This knowledge led me to wonder how treatments might better address issues of culture, and I began to see the development of these manuals as part of my future career. Moreover, as one of the few Spanish-speaking therapists in my community, I continually received referrals for Latino clients, and I realized that Latinos have limited access to culturally competent mental health services. This not only motivated me to work in various clinical settings where I was able to apply my linguistic and cultural knowledge but also refined my career goal to the development of treatments tailored for the Latino community.

Although I had thought of myself primarily as a clinician in the past, research is now central to my career goals. Through clinical work, I started to develop research questions concerning the interpersonal antecedents of maladaptive behavior. My master's thesis examined the differential prediction of perceived peer rejection and victimization on adolescent psychological outcomes. After completing my master's, I received a grant to pursue friendship processes associated with adolescent depression. I am especially interested in understanding the quantification of dyadic processes and how children and adolescents internalize and cope with interpersonal distress. Given the interpersonal focus of various cultural groups, I see this research in line with the development of culturally tailored interventions for children, adolescents, and families.

In addition to my clinical and research interests, my experiences teaching and supervising have led me to hope that one day I will pursue a career as a professor in a university setting. In my 4th year, I became the advanced student graduate supervisor for our department's child practicum. Providing supervision not only enhanced my own clinical and case conceptualization skills but also afforded me the opportunity to teach others how to think clinically. I greatly enjoyed being able to challenge students and shape how they understood clinical phenomena and interventions. For example, in the application of a parenting manual, one of the students failed to recognize clinical moments that might have led the parents to a deeper understanding of their parenting. Instead, the student mechanically led the parents through the prescribed tasks. In the use of clinical manuals, I find it is more important to be true to the theoretical mechanisms of change than to the specific tasks. I helped her notice these "clinical windows" and understand how the manual conceptualized change processes, leading her to be able to use these opportunities to achieve change.

Throughout graduate school, I have taken advantage of opportunities to grow professionally, and I hope to continue to do so during internship. I look forward to internship training that will provide me with (a) additional multicultural training with Latino populations; (b) continued exposure to a variety of theoretical orientations; and (c) an opportunity to learn evidence-based treatments for adolescent depression. I believe these goals are essential to my career objectives, and I am excited that such experiences appear to be available at your training site.

More Sample Essay 1 Responses

Please note: All biographical and other identifying information has been removed from the sample essays shown here. Remember, these additional examples are not necessarily ideal or flawless, but they represent the types of essays that former applicants have submitted.

Sample Essay 1A. I approached psychology very seriously as an undergraduate student, and I arrived at the University of [State] eager to begin my training as a clinical psychologist. I did not anticipate, however, just how out of place I would initially feel. It had not occurred to me that being the youngest of my cohort, the sole individual from the Deep South, and the one student who was the first in their family to attend college would set me apart. For the first time in my life, I questioned whether I was prepared for the endeavors before me. I did not dress like my classmates, come from a comparable background, or even use a similar vocabulary. I imagined that these differences surely would create a problem. What I found, in contrast, is that my differences contribute to my strengths as a clinical psychologist. My background and the individuality it helped to shape remain important influences and have allowed me to retain *myself* as a tool in the therapy room.

The science *and* art of clinical psychology are what attracted me to the field. The complexity involved in "getting it right" and balancing the two aspects of clinical practice is a never-ending pursuit that maintains my excitement for this work. My clinical training has been firmly grounded in cognitive behavior theory and developmental theory, and I am committed to the integration of science and practice. In addition, I believe that evidence-based conceptualization and treatment are informed optimally by flexible thinking that is based on the integration of relevant theoretical perspectives. Thus, augmenting my training with an increased understanding of other theoretical orientations is necessary to strengthen my identity and subsequent practice as a clinical psychologist. Indeed, such additional training is a primary goal of my internship year.

My clinical interests evolved from my undergraduate research experiences with delinquent youth. I realized that these children had not been troubled since birth, and I wanted to understand how some youth succumb to risk while others remain resilient. I also became keenly aware that the services these youth received typically were insufficient, and I wondered about the most effective ways to treat children and adolescents. Thus, my research naturally informed my clinical interests and thinking. Since then, I have been particularly invested in working with underserved and at-risk populations, with a specific interest in how contextual factors may exacerbate or ameliorate their adjustment. To this end, I have sought training experiences with children and adults from diverse racial, ethnic, and socioeconomic backgrounds. Also, I have worked to increase my familiarity with the multiple sources that can potentially serve as points of intervention, including various treatment modalities, therapeutic settings, and consultation sources. This breadth of experience has been invaluable in informing my professional growth.

I view my clinical internship as a crucial step in my professional development, and my goal is to build on the foundation of my training thus far. Thus, I am interested in continued work with underserved populations, particularly youth and their families. I envision refining and expanding upon my skills in assessment and intervention via training that is informed by a range of theoretical orientations and exposure to diverse client populations.

Sample Essay 1B. As I ponder my life thus far, a quotation by William Hazlitt (1778) comes to mind: "A strong passion . . . will insure success, for the desire of the end will point out the means." *Ambition, passion, service, motivation,* and *persistence* are words that have dominated my life's work and created my life's path. These sustaining qualities have been both influenced and maintained by significant individuals and by experiences throughout the years.

I am the oldest of a family of four children raised in a small, poor rural town. Heavily influenced by a Russian Judaic background and Native American spirituality, our family struggled to fit into the social mold. Despite the obstacles that surrounded my childhood years, my parents were supportive and encouraged me to strive to reach my full potential. My family's constant belief that you can create your destiny, as well as their belief in my talents and ability to contribute to the healing profession, planted the first seeds of motivation and passion for service.

Growing up in a family of healers, I quickly discovered the value of providing assistance to those in need. Thus, when I was in sixth grade I made the decision to pursue a career as a psychologist. In college, my first experience in the field was working with emotionally disturbed and sexually abused young women. In addition, it was at this time that a close friend was assaulted. I saw clearly for the first time the power of a psychologist's work, and my commitment to women's issues, trauma recovery, and my career path was solidified. In continued pursuit of my passion and ambition for service, I sought a master's degree. It was during my master's program that fervor for research and for the substance use field developed. However, this program also created a thirst for more knowledge and experience. Thus, I enrolled in a doctoral program in counseling psychology.

I have developed my skills, interests, and identity as a mental health professional through a variety of mentoring relationships and educational and training experiences. These relationships and experiences have helped me gather the strength and fortitude to trust myself and to utilize my strengths. They have also helped maintain my commitment, dedication, and passion for psychology. In addition, my relationships and experiences have also taught me the necessity in balancing my career aspirations with a personal life. To rejuvenate, I enjoy time with my animals, hiking, meditating, or reading a favorite philosopher. Additionally, I love to travel, to dance, and to participate in a variety of advocacy groups.

Hence, not only have my passion and commitment to my work been unwavering, they have been the impetus for a variety of meaningful professional and personal experiences. Thus far, I feel proud of where my passion and dedication have brought me and feel excited about where they might take me. I look forward to the prospect of having them bring the opportunity to personally introduce myself to you.

Sample Essay 1C. I certainly cannot say that I expected to become a clinical psychologist from an early age. Indeed, growing up in a hard-working family in [City, State], where my father and older brothers are mechanics, a career in psychology was well off my anticipated path. However, I was introduced to clinical psychology as a high school senior and was immediately fascinated by the models I learned about that explained different facets of human behavior. These models greatly facilitated my understanding of the functions, orderliness, and predictability of many behaviors, and the applications appeared endless. More recently, I have learned to use clinical psychology not only as a means to understand the actions of others but, more important, also as a vehicle for helping to improve people's functioning and mental health, which I think is really the most valuable thing one has.

The significance of accurately evaluating and treating psychopathology became particularly clear to me during a college internship in a locked psychiatric unit for violent inpatients during a semester abroad. This unique experience confirmed my interest in clinical work but also triggered a whole set of questions in my mind that remain at the center of my clinical and research interests: Why do some people repeatedly engage in aggressive behaviors, while others are compelled to hurt themselves? Why are some virtually paralyzed by anxiety and depression? How can we change the behaviors of those who want help? What about those who do not? After consulting my supervisors and visiting the library, I was intrigued and motivated to learn that the answers to such crucial questions remain, to a large extent, unknown.

Over the next several years, I deliberately sought out a wide range of clinical and research positions in the mental health field that approached the understanding and treatment of these problems from a number of different perspectives. Through each of these unique experiences, I consistently realized the value and importance of using systematic observation and evaluation as a means of studying these phenomena and developing effective treatments. Consequently, I chose to attend the doctoral program at [State] University because of its strong commitment to the scientist–practitioner training model. This training has taught me not only to be a consumer of clinical research but also to use scientific methods to continually evaluate the treatments I provide and to actively contribute to the larger scientific and clinical community. For instance, I have completed several clinically relevant studies on the development and treatment of aggression, anxiety, and suicidal behaviors. Moreover, my dissertation research, funded by the National Institute of Mental Health (NIMH), is focused on evaluating the effectiveness of a therapy preparation component, which I developed based on recent research conducted at our clinic, to increase participation and therapeutic change in child therapy. Such an interaction between science and practice is what continues to excite me about this work and is a consistent theme in my approach to clinical and research activities.

I look forward to internship as a valuable opportunity to continue to obtain the best training experience possible to strengthen the foundation on which I will build my career as a clinician, researcher, and teacher. I am strongly interested in the internship program at [Your Site] because it offers the most logical continuation of my scientist-practitioner training, as well as exciting opportunities to expand on my knowledge of evidenced-based treatments and to continue to apply these interventions to a wide variety of clients (children, adolescents, and adults) in diverse settings (outpatient and inpatient). I hope I will have the opportunity to receive this training at [Your Site] and to be as much of a benefit to the internship program as I know it will be to me.

THEORETICAL ORIENTATION, ESSAY 2

Please describe your theoretical orientation and how this influences your approach to case conceptualization and intervention. You may use de-identified case material to illustrate your points if you choose.

Essays 2 and 3 often are regarded as exercises in which one feels pulled to give the "right" answer. In other words, these essays sometimes seem to be academic or evaluative, and you may feel motivated to demonstrate your knowledge from coursework. However, this is not an optimal approach. Again, consider how to make yourself a unique applicant and help the reader think of you as someone the reader would be excited to work with in supervision. For example, defining cognitive behavior therapy in Essay 2 is of no help to those who read the essays. They understand the basic tenets of all the major theoretical orientations and do not need brief lessons in them or a demonstration that you know them. Although it is important to demonstrate knowledge of the field and of psychological theory and practice in these essays, we suggest that it is more important to discuss your personal opinions, beliefs, and practices in the essay. It is OK to take a stand and discuss your beliefs. Remember, you are applying for a training position, and your openness to learning, growing, and further developing your theoretical orientation is important.

Essay 2 is used to help you explain the type of training models you were exposed to in your graduate program and the type of training you would like to receive on internship. You may wish to convey past experiences by using a case example, or not. You should most certainly discuss future training in an explicit way. If you have chosen a particular site because of its theoretical orientation, then say so! And—very important—integrate some statements regarding your goals and discuss the manner in which your case conceptualization skills will both fit the site and be further cultivated by the training experiences that the site has to offer. You don't need a different Essay 2 for every site, but if you picked your sites with consistent goals in mind, a broad statement about what kind of training/supervision you are looking for during internship will work for all your sites.

You may use some of these questions to help you write this essay.

- How do you approach cases theoretically? Be clear about your theoretical orientation to your clinical work. Why do you have this orientation, and what more would you like to learn?
- What is your approach to assessment? Do you consider differential diagnoses? Do you explore themes in the pattern of your client's relationships or the style in which these experiences are discussed by the client? Were there early experiences that were pivotal in shaping your assessment approach?
- How do you proceed with treatment? Do you measure relevant outcomes as you progress? Do you establish treatment goals? How do you know when treatment is over? What are your beliefs about treatment orientations, and how do you think the future of field will deal with disparate orientations?
- What are your strengths and weaknesses in case conceptualization? Yes, it is OK to discuss weaknesses (i.e., areas for which you would like to receive additional training). Internship is a training experience, and you should explain how you would like to be trained.

Try to carry the same themes you discussed in your autobiographical essay into Essay 2. This is important to help you demonstrate and reiterate your training goals.

Essay 2 will also take several drafts, mostly because it is normal for graduate students to have had little time to reflect on this topic before the time comes to write this essay, and some reflection is needed to complete this essay well.

Many believe that this essay offers a unique window into what you will be like as a supervisee. What is your "take" on the field? What unique perspectives, debates, approaches, or points of confusion will you bring with you into the internship supervisor's office on your first day? Note that it is not expected that you already have all the answers and that you are fully developed as a psychologist already. You are applying for a training position. Thus, it may be a good idea for you to use this essay to talk about the training issues that you find most intriguing. Perhaps you will note your burgeoning interest in third-wave therapies and your desire to learn more. You might discuss the limitations you have experienced in your practicum experiences and how they helped you realize the value of a diverse clinical skill toolbox. Or maybe you will review how your particular perspective as a psychologist (from Essay 1) helps change your approach to assessment or therapy. Whatever you choose to discuss, try to offer some examples that will help the reader of this essay to get a sense of what you are like in the therapy (or assessment) room, and what it may be like to discuss cases with you during an internship year.

Sample Responses for Essay 2

Sample Essay 2A. My approach to case conceptualization and treatment is an integrative process heavily influenced by four main factors: (a) the developmental psychopathology perspective that has enriched my understanding of how normal and abnormal functioning develops across the lifespan, (b) the cognitive behavioral framework within which I have been predominantly trained, (c) my strong commitment to the integration of science and practice, and (d) my pursuit of breadth and depth in understanding the clients with whom I work.

When a client has been referred for treatment, my initial focus is on comprehensively assessing who this person is and how she developed the presenting problems. In doing so, the developmental psychopathology perspective as well as Bronfenbrenner's bioecological model have taught me to consider the multiple systems that may be contributing to the client's primary concerns. This is particularly important when working with a child or adolescent and includes consideration of her particular point in development. Thus, assessment focuses on individual characteristics (e.g., thinking and behavioral patterns); the family system, peers, and other important social influences; and the broader cultural community within which the client is embedded. My approach also emphasizes the interdependence of these multiple levels, leading to consideration of how my client impacts and contributes to her environment. This recognition of bidirectionality further helps me understand my client's unique strengths and weaknesses as they apply to questions of minimizing risk and enhancing resiliency, and this assessment directly impacts my treatment plan.

After a rich conceptualization has been developed during the initial assessment phase, I begin constructing a plan for intervention. Given my allegiance to the integration of science and practice in my clinical work, the initial treatment plan often involves consulting the relevant research literatures as needed. Additionally, I often consult evidence-based manuals that have demonstrated effectiveness with populations having backgrounds and circumstances similar to my client's. Given that the cognitive behavioral framework has been studied, and more readily applied, to the treatment of psychopathology than any other approach, cognitive behavior therapy often provides the foundation for building an effective treatment strategy. Furthermore, given my emphasis on the multiple systems involved in development and change, I also carefully consider how to incorporate relevant systemic factors, whether directly or indirectly in the therapeutic process.

My view of psychotherapy is that the process is an ever-evolving one that involves ongoing assessment and feedback from the client to maximize treatment gains. This continual process often leads to consideration of how other theoretical perspectives can augment my conceptualization and thinking, and I have found it extremely beneficial to broaden the scope of my theoretical orientation to gain greater depth in understanding my clients. Thus, dynamic and interpersonal theories have bolstered my understanding of how psychopathology develops and manifests across the life course, as well as how the therapeutic process itself can be influenced by a person's history. The field of psychopharmacology has augmented my understanding of the interplay between biology and psychology. Multicultural theories have enhanced my awareness and sensitivity to some of the more subtle ways in which culture and identity can impact a client. I view these, as well as other relevant perspectives, as essential tools in adding to the breadth and depth necessary to optimally understand and treat clients with the care, respect, and expertise they deserve. Thus, my goal for the internship year is to continue refining and expanding upon my conceptualization and treatment skills by gaining increased exposure, understanding, and comfort with multiple theoretical perspectives.

Sample Essay 2B. Innate empathy, genuine concern, and compassion are personal attributes that I bring to my role as a trainee. These characteristics have been the foundation on which my clinical strengths have emerged and continue to develop. I am able to aptly identify client strengths and resiliencies that can be used as anchoring points for productive client change, leaving clients with a sense of empowerment and dignity in situations that may appear hopeless, stressful, overwhelming, or defeating. I seek to establish a cooperative environment that allows for the exchange of ideas and expertise in the therapy process. I use diagnosis as a mechanism for client change and insight.

Rather than offering a diagnosis as the answer to the client's problem situation, I prefer to use diagnosis as a springboard for generative therapeutic conversation. This approach is consistent with my theoretical orientation.

Postmodern assumptions that include social constructivism and narrative approaches to therapy inform the way I think about and talk with clients. I organize my thinking through the metaphors of narration (or storytelling) and social construction. I conceptualize problems as being separate from the person experiencing the difficulties. Many problems are stories that clients construct through social interaction. These socially constructed realities provide the beliefs, practices, words, and experiences from which clients create their life stories and constitute themselves. The meanings that clients attribute to the events and experiences in their lives create their reality. Because meaning is created through individuals in conversation, new meaning and a new reality can be introduced by changing the stories clients tell themselves. Every client has his or her own version of truth with its own inherent logic. Clients interpret their experiences based upon their version of truth, and these realities, or truths, can be organized, maintained, or changed through modifying the types of conversations in which clients are engaged or exposed.

Similarly, assessment can be useful in offering one possible life story for clients to accept, reject, or change. Given the dynamic nature of assessments, these tools can help provide direction for the client and therapist in determining which aspects of the client's story they wish to retain and which they would like to change. From a consultative perspective, helping clients create alternate meanings for symptoms creates opportunities for change and intervention rather than restricting options. For me, good clinical interviews determine the appropriate diagnostic tests to administer and the subsequent use of those tests in understanding and treating the client's presenting problems. I do not use any predetermined set of tests for every client I see, as the nature of the client's problems and needs will dictate the tests and interventions used.

Sample Essay 2C. My approach to case conceptualization, evaluation, and treatment planning is primarily behavioral and cognitive behavioral in nature and is strongly influenced by the principles of learning (e.g., operant and classical conditioning paradigms). Although learning theory is most often associated with behavioral and cognitive-behavioral treatments, the basic elements of this theoretical framework are pervasive in cognitive, psychodynamic, humanistic, and other treatment approaches, strengthening the appeal and the applicability of this approach.

The first, and perhaps most important, step in my application of this approach to a clinical case is the use of comprehensive, reliable, and valid assessments that draw on multiple methods and informants and that continue to test, inform, and guide the case conceptualization and intervention plan throughout treatment. My next step is the collaborative development of a clear and specific list of presenting problems and an evaluation of the clinical severity and impairment associated with each problem. At the center of my case conceptualization is a generation of hypotheses about the function of each problem behavior, including an analysis of factors that may be causing or maintaining these problems (e.g., antecedents and consequences of each behavior) and about the interrelation of the presenting problems.

My treatment plan follows directly from my primary case conceptualization. On the most basic level, whatever maladaptive learning has occurred must be "unlearned" (e.g., an association between a feared object and anxiety is weakened via exposure) and whatever adaptive learning has not occurred must be learned (e.g., prosocial behavior is increased when followed by positive reinforcement). As assessment and treatment are inseparable elements from my perspective, the continuous evaluation of the target problems is a critical component of my approach. The information provided by frequent and continued assessments is used to test the effectiveness of the intervention and to modify my conceptualization and treatment plan as necessary. In addition, my treatment plan incorporates evidence-based treatment techniques or treatment packages when available and is based directly on the principles of learning whenever possible.

I particularly enjoy working from a learning perspective because this approach is straightforward, flexible, parsimonious, widely applicable, and evidence based. I look forward to receiving additional training in the use of evidence-based evaluation and treatment procedures during internship. Indeed, I am uniquely interested in the internship program at [site] because of the attention given to such approaches in didactic instruction, clinical training, and case supervision, as well as the rich opportunities to interact with clinicians and supervisors working from a wide range of case conceptualization approaches to which I have had less exposure (such as psychodynamic and interpersonal approaches), as these are my main goals for the internship year. Moreover, the application of such approaches to the treatment of impulsive, anxious, and depressed children and adolescents, such as that offered in the [Site Center] rotations at the Institute for the Study of Psychological Service and the Anxiety and Mood Disorders Service, are a direct match with my previous training and current interests, and I look forward to the chance to learn more about these opportunities.

DIVERSITY EXPERIENCE, ESSAY 3

Please describe your experience and training in work with diverse populations. Your discussion should display explicitly the manner in which multicultural/diversity issues influence your clinical practice and case conceptualization.

You likely have discussed the importance of diversity and cultural competence in your classes, and you likely recognize that you can overlay a cultural framework onto virtually every activity you engage in as a psychologist. This essay gives you an opportunity to discuss your thoughts and experiences regarding issues of diversity in greater detail.

An essay summarizing all your clients who are demographically different from you may not be the best use of this essay. Much of this information could be gleaned from your AAPI and CV, and this approach does not reflect your thinking and your development as a psychologist-in-training.

Some applicants tell a story of a particular experience with a client in which they had a significant insight regarding the importance of cultural competence that forever changed their approach to clinical work. This may yield a more useful and interesting essay, but keep in mind that this approach is quite common and does not often differentiate applicants.

In fact, the vast majority of essays read something like this:

> I believe multiculturalism is important. Indeed, I have worked with many clients who are demographically different from myself, including *a*, *b*, *c*, *d*, *e*, and even *f*. Here is a case example: I once had a client who was different than me on variable *x*. They said one thing, I thought another. Then, I realized that I had to consider variable *x*. I had an epiphany! Once we talked about variable *x*, it changed my conceptualization on this case and we all lived happily ever after. I want to continue to think about diversity training on internship.

If this is what your first draft sounds like, please start again.

An approach to this essay that most certainly will differentiate your application is to discuss something that is unique to you—that is, your beliefs, your thoughts, and your ideas. In addition to the types of messages conveyed above (i.e., discussing past experiences or pivotal moments), you also can use this essay to discuss your thoughts regarding what you believe to be the future needs in the field, how you believe your training would benefit from specific types of experiences, and what specific competencies you feel you have developed regarding cultural competence. How could, should, or would you incorporate these ideas into clinical practice and research? Similarly, as you increasingly have become a more culturally competent individual who is sensitive

44 ■ INTERNSHIPS IN PSYCHOLOGY

to the range of diversity issues, what has surprised you the most about what you have learned about yourself in this process? What are you particularly proud of, or what are some areas that have been a struggle for you?

Consider addressing the following questions when planning your essay.

- What does diversity mean to you?
- What situation did you experience when you recognized that diversity was important to consider? Remember, *diversity* can refer to demographic, geographic, or ideological heterogeneity among your past clients.
- Have your experiences led you to develop specific (primary or supplemental) training goals related to diversity?
- How do these goals match the opportunities offered at this training site? What are your multicultural counseling competencies? What are your weaknesses in this area?

Sample Responses for Essay 3

Sample Essay 3A. Embracing a multicultural perspective is an integral component of every case conceptualization and treatment plan. This has been salient particularly in my work with underserved populations, but it is equally relevant to every individual because we all develop within a cultural context. Thus, viewing clients through a cultural lens allows for greater awareness of the multitude of risk and protective factors that may be contributing to their clinical presentations. This does not mean that aspects of culture always play a primary role in explaining the development of psychopathology. However, a critical part of all assessments is careful consideration of the relevant contextual factors that may have important implications for treatment. Some features of a client's cultural context are more salient than others and have clear links with a person's adjustment, such as how an individual's race may lead to experiences with discrimination. Equally important, however, is consideration of the subtler ways in which a person's culture may affect functioning, such as how a person's cultural upbringing may inform the most effective therapeutic modality or how a person's gender or race may affect his symptom presentation.

Although I believe that it is essential to situate each client within a multicultural framework, I also think that it is extremely important to recognize that the guiding principles of a multicultural model should not be used as a means for stereotyping and categorizing to simplify a client's unique development and presentation. Thus, it is essential to acknowledge differences but not let that unduly influence case conceptualization and interpretation. Rather, a multicultural framework should allow for an enriched understanding of the complexity of a client's motives, strengths, and vulnerabilities. Intragroup variations are a critical component of such a framework.

I have a strong commitment to issues of diversity, and I view related education and training as an integral component of my work. I have sought experiences with diverse clinical populations, and I also have chosen to focus my independent research projects on the adjustment of African American youth from single-mother homes. In addition, I have been actively involved in my program's diversity committee, diversity-related workshops, and minority-focused seminars. In my opinion, multicultural training is not something that can be learned in a single course or in working with a single client.

Rather, it is an ever-evolving process that continues throughout professional development. Moreover, part of the learning experience has been in recognizing the cultural context within which I have developed so that I can continue to develop a greater awareness of my own biases and how they influence the ways in which I interpret and respond to clients. Thus, continued exposure to diverse client populations is one of my primary objectives for internship.

Sample Essay 3B. I believe it is essential—particularly as an individual aspiring to a career of service to the distressed—to remain sensitive, always, to multicultural issues. As a member of several categories of the majority culture who has benefited from a lifetime of relative privilege, visible and invisible, there was a time when I was far more naïve regarding this responsibility. Several life experiences, clinical contacts, and formal trainings have proven invaluable and transformative for me in my path toward multicultural competence in my clinical practice. One stands out. Over the summer before applying to graduate school, I lived in Arusha, Tanzania, and worked at an orphanage and school for children. As one of a small handful of "mzungu," or White people, living among a homogenous Black population, I had never felt so constantly and intensely scrutinized by the people around me for my outward appearance. When I walked to work every morning, a growing chorus of children would trail, shouting, "Mzungu! Mzungu!" I had never fully felt the pervasive and exhausting experience of stereotype threat until, on several occasions, good friends asked me questions like, "As a White person, what do you think about . . .?" or "What does it feel like to be White?" This experience and a few invaluable others have provided me with rare opportunities to travel as a "tourist" within a dramatically different cultural identity. Although it seems obvious that one's cultural characteristics are most visible against a starkly contrasted majority culture's, it is difficult to know how profoundly this can be felt unless one experiences it.

This kind of experience has helped shape and give depth to my clinical work with diverse populations. Two principles most prominently underlie my current approach to multiculturally informed practice. First, I believe that multiculturalism must be defined as an almost infinitely broad construct. In some senses there are aspects of every individual's cultural background and identity that may distinguish him or her even from immediate family members. (For example, as the youngest and only male child in a family of six I need no reminders of how differently my sisters and I have conceptualized our upbringing.) In essence, everyone has a unique story. Of course, individuals who would seem to have obvious differences in their evident culture—across such categories as gender, sexual identity/orientation, ethnicity, or socioeconomic status—may share far more similarities than differences. An important lesson for my clinical practice is the realization that it is never safe to make assumptions, either about the background experiences or cultural identities of the individual before me or about the ways in which each individual's unique strengths and vulnerabilities may (or may not) be shaped by culture.

Logically extending this point relates to the second principle guiding my clinical practice. The concept of "multicultural competence" is far from an enlightened state at which one aspires to arrive. Rather, it is an attitude and orientation to clinical work. It is not enough, for example, for a competent practitioner to educate him- or herself about diverse populations and phenomena within them. (In fact, the use of such knowledge derived from groups must be used cautiously so as not to obscure potentially more important individual differences.) True competence entails a lifelong process of "listening" carefully and developing greater awareness, both of the client's background and of one's own cultural schema and biases.

Continuing my own development as a multiculturally competent clinician is one of my major goals for internship. It is my hope that this year will present opportunities for more focused and varied exposure to clients with diverse backgrounds and identities across developmental stages. An internship within an urban medical center, medical school, or consortium would be the ideal setting to accomplish this goal.

Sample Essay 3C. I am fortunate to have had a wealth of clinical and training experiences with diverse populations up to this point in my career, and I look forward to building on these experiences during internship. At [State] University, diversity training is an integral part of the course curriculum and clinical training. For instance, we have a weekly, semester-long seminar series focusing on clinical research relevant to ethnic and cultural diversity presented by eminent researchers from around the country. In addition, issues of socioeconomic, ethnic, and cultural diversity have been explicitly addressed in each of my clinical practica at [State] University, through which I evaluated and treated a diverse client population from the [City, State, Area]. Also, as an active member of my department's diversity committee, I am helping to develop methods of diversifying our own graduate student population and training experience.

The clinical experiences I had before graduate school also provided the opportunity to work with unique and diverse populations. For instance, in Europe, I worked at a psychiatric hospital that served a large, urban catchment area and that had a violent, severely ill, and socioculturally diverse population. In [City], my experiences ranged from working for a corporate managed health care organization serving professional clientele to working as an intake clinician at [Outpatient Service], a homeless shelter for an under-21 population consisting primarily of low-income minority adolescents. These experiences with truly diverse populations have prepared me well for future work in a range of clinical settings.

As a result of my training and clinical experiences, issues of ethnic, cultural, and socioeconomic diversity influence my case conceptualization, assessment, and treatment procedures in several ways. First, I routinely evaluate whether (and how) a client or family's cultural beliefs influence his or her view of the presenting problems. For example, ethnic and cultural differences in parenting style (e.g., permissiveness vs. strictness) have been well documented and can often influence a parent's perception of his or her child's behavior problems. Second, I similarly evaluate whether a client or family's cultural beliefs influence their view of psychotherapy in general or the specific treatment plan in particular. For instance, some of my research has demonstrated that African American and Latino families tend to view psychotherapy as less credible than do European American families and that this view may lead to decreased participation in treatment. Third, I evaluate whether a client or family's cultural beliefs influence the method of treatment delivery. For instance, I recently worked with a family from the Dominican Republic in which the success of the intervention was greatly facilitated by actively involving the father in treatment planning and implementation, as he was the head of the household and yielded a strong influence over the rules of the house and the disciplinary practices with the children. I believe that a failure to recognize this cultural dynamic could have led to a lack of treatment adherence or attrition from treatment altogether.

I believe it is essential for my development as a clinician and researcher that I continue to receive training and experiences in the treatment of diverse populations. Indeed, this diversity is one of the many things I enjoy about [City, State] and is one of the reasons I am enthusiastic about the possibility of participating in the internship program at [Site].

Please describe your research experience and interests.

This essay may not seem applicable to all. Some applicants have already decided that their dissertation will be their last involvement in research activities. Others hope to gain substantial research experience on internship. Either way, you had major research milestones while in graduate school, so everyone should be able to write a good version of this essay that demonstrates his or her understanding of psychological theory, an empiricist approach, and an ability to translate hypotheses and findings into clinical implications.

You should approach this essay by discussing your research program. Start with a few statements regarding your philosophy about how human behavior and/or psychopathology "works." An overarching statement about your philosophy, interests, or beliefs will differentiate this statement from a mere list of your research projects in graduate school. In the paragraphs that follow, you will want to discuss each of your past graduate-level research experiences; the themes of your research program; your dissertation, including its (current and expected) completion status; and your interests regarding research training before and after internship. You also may wish to discuss how these research experiences have informed your clinical work. Provide a specific example or perhaps discuss a theory with clinical application.

You do not want this essay to sound as though you are applying for a research assistant position. A detailed list of your responsibilities (e.g., "I conducted 100 structured interviews!") is not as valuable as a discussion of your interests, the findings in your research, and their clinical implications.

Sample Responses for Essay 4

Sample Essay 4A. My program of research has evolved from my interest in the frameworks articulated by the developmental psychopathology perspective and Bronfenbrenner's bioecological model. Thus, I have collaborated on a number of projects that include consideration of the multiple dynamic systems that influence child development, including individual, family, and broader environmental factors. Moreover, I particularly am interested in understanding the development and treatment of internalizing behaviors in at-risk youth from understudied populations. Both my master's and dissertation projects focused on the ways in which neighborhood context influences the association between self-regulation difficulties and depression in African American youth.

Findings from my master's thesis revealed that disadvantaged neighborhoods exacerbated the relation between early maltreatment difficulties and depression in girls. Thus, in an effort to extend this preliminary investigation, my dissertation (to be completed prior to internship) further examines this association by including both objectively and subjectively defined indicators of neighborhood effects, as well as further examination of gender differences. Accordingly, my dissertation aims to address how variations in neighborhood assessment similarly or differently moderate the link between self-regulation difficulties and depression. Research such as this is necessary to identify the ways in which individual and environmental systems may interact to exacerbate, or alternatively, ameliorate a child's risk for psychopathology. My dissertation therefore will provide important clinical implications for African American youth, their families, and their communities. My hope is that this research will enhance the implementation of successful intervention efforts, as well as aid in the accurate identification of subgroups most in need of our treatment programs.

In addition to my independent research endeavors, I have collaborated with my advisor on a number of papers and presentations that broadly focus on the family as a context for studying both parental and child adjustment (please see my CV). For over a year, I also have served as the project coordinator of a grant-funded, community-based study examining the role of extended family members in the psychosocial adjustment of African American youth. I have been fortunate to be involved in virtually every aspect of the project, and my primary responsibilities include recruiting families, training and managing staff, and conducting the interviews. My integral involvement has been an invaluable learning experience and has provided an excellent model for how to design, implement, and execute a successful community-based research program.

I believe that sound clinical practice must be informed by research that addresses questions of how and why. Similarly, rich clinical experiences are the mechanisms through which meaningful research is fostered. Ultimately, I am interested in producing research that aids in the development of theoretically derived, culturally sensitive, multisystemic prevention and intervention programs. Accordingly, my hope for the internship year is that I will gain exposure to clinical experiences that will expand my knowledge base, refine my hypotheses, and incite questions that lead to further exploration of the multiple interdependent contexts within which youth develop.

Sample Essay 4B. As someone who embraces the scientist–practitioner model, my clinical interests and research interests are complementary. I have sought clinical training and a degree specialty in dual diagnosis, with trauma and substance use being the main foci. In addition, I have conducted research on, among other things, correlates of substance use and trauma, motivation and substance use, treatment utilization and substance use, and gender and sensation-seeking differences in substance use.

When searching for a topic for my dissertation, I attempted to merge my identities as a researcher and clinician. Consequently, I have a dissertation goal of documenting the differential effects of rape among addicted women on treatment utilization, treatment motivation, perceived barriers to treatment, and problem severity. I believe that there is a lack of research and knowledge of the difference rape makes in treatment for women in the addiction field. The purpose of my dissertation is twofold. First, I intend to show that rape decreases motivation for addiction treatment, causes more perceived barriers to treatment, decreases treatment utilization, and increases different types of problem severity. Second, I intend to explore some qualitative questions regarding their motivation for treatment. The latter section intends to explore more of the interplay of their symptoms and their motivation for various types of treatment. The main motivation construct in this study is based on Prochaska and DiClemente's model. I have chosen to apply for a grant to fund my project and to utilize a publication format for my dissertation write-up, and I intend to have at least two manuscripts suitable for publication as an end result.

I have developed a strong knowledge base in statistical and research methodology as a result of my educational career. I have worked on many research projects, performing a myriad of duties ranging from working with participants, to data entry, to questionnaire development, to data analysis. Consequently, I have developed a strong research identity. Additionally, as a scientist–practitioner, I believe that research should inform clinical practice and clinical practice should inform research. Therefore, I am committed to publishing and presenting results of my psychological research at national and local conferences. I am currently working on multiple manuscripts that will be submitted for publication prior to my beginning internship. In addition, I am committed to publishing the results of my dissertation. I am dedicated to presenting and publishing my work because I believe it will provide valuable information to clinicians and other researchers.

As someone who aspires to future research in trauma, posttraumatic stress, and substance use, as related to treatment engagement, completion, and efficacy, I believe I can further develop my research skills through additional research and clinical mentorship. Therefore, I continuously seek clinical and research experiences related to these interests to help inform my research and clinical future.

Sample Essay 4C. My research focuses broadly on the etiologies, assessment, and treatment of impulsive, aggressive, and self-injurious behaviors in children and adolescents. These behaviors are widespread and often cause serious impairment and physical harm, yet they are not well studied or understood, particularly in children and adolescents. Given the limited research on these topics to date, much of my research has attempted to answer fundamental questions related to the development and assessment of these conditions. For instance, my master's thesis examined affective, behavioral, and cognitive aspects of child suicide. Other studies I have completed examined more extreme forms of impulsive and aggressive behavior such as parent-directed physical aggression in clinic-referred children and severe acts of violence in Vietnam veterans.

Although these and other studies of mine have explored a range of factors associated with aggressive and self-injurious behaviors, I have become particularly interested in the role of emotion dysregulation in the occurrence of these behaviors. For instance, I found that the primary reason given for self-mutilation by adolescent psychiatric inpatients is that it serves to help regulate their emotional experiences. Also, frustration intolerance, a related construct, was a significant predictor of parent-directed physical aggression in children in another study. The significant role of emotion dysregulation in the occurrence of aggressive and self-injurious behaviors has led to a secondary interest in other conditions characterized by problems with emotion regulation, such as anxiety and depressive disorders. Obviously, there is still much work to be done in addressing fundamental questions related to the assessment and prediction of impulsive, aggressive, and self-injurious behaviors, as well as on emotion dysregulation, and one arm of my research will continue to focus in these areas.

More recently, the scope of my research has expanded to focus on the treatment of impulsive and aggressive behaviors in children and adolescents. I completed a second master's thesis that included a review of recent progress in the treatment of child conduct problems and concluded that there is a significant gap in our understanding of the mechanisms through which these treatments work or what factors moderate their efficacy or effectiveness. My dissertation, for which I received a NIMH National Research Service Award, is addressing one factor that pertains to the latter issue: namely, the role of parents' participation (i.e., attendance and adherence) in their child's treatment. More specifically, I am conducting (a) a descriptive study examining several potential predictors (e.g., parent motivation and expectancies for treatment) and outcomes of parent participation, as well as (b) a randomized, controlled clinical trial testing a brief (one-session) intervention designed to increase parent participation by identifying and removing potential barriers to parent participation at the start of treatment. At a very basic level, the efficacy of our current treatments—particularly those that are skills based—may be weakened if clients do not attend or adhere to treatment. Accordingly, this line of research may produce a means of improving the therapeutic outcome of a range of clinical conditions and client populations.

Given my interest in continuing these, and related, lines of clinical research, I am extremely excited about the possibility of participating in the [Site] child and adolescent internship program. Several of the clinical rotations offered, such as those at the Institute for the Study of Psychological Service and the Anxiety and Mood Disorders Service, as well as the opportunity to work in the psychiatric inpatient unit, match closely with my goals for clinical training as well as with my current and future research interests.

COVER LETTER: "SELL" THE FIT

Although no one part of the AAPI or the materials that you submit is more important than the others, the cover letter is usually the first document read. Therefore, as the introduction to you and your application file, it helps reviewers decide how closely they will review the rest of your application and what to look for. Your cover letter will either entice the reader to delve into your full application or it will cause them to file your materials in their "no" folder and move on to the next application. This is your chance to set a tone and reveal some of your personality and professionalism through your writing style. As such, you want to make a positive initial impression by providing an engaging, high-level overview of your application, and share any information that may not otherwise fit within the AAPI or essays.

How do you write an attention-getting cover letter and persuade the reader to want to learn more about you? First and foremost, think about how you can distinguish yourself as a top candidate, especially if you are applying to sites that are more competitive (e.g., receive many applications for few spots) and are inundated with applications. Begin by being both succinct and deliberate with every word you use. Obviously, there should be no spelling or grammar errors and your letter needs to read in a logical, flowing sequence. Apart from precision, your letter must be compelling. This is accomplished through personalization and customization. Detached, neutral, and nonspecific form letters are boring and give the impression that there is nothing you find exciting, unique, or interesting about the site that draws you to it. In other words, use your cover letter to connect with the reviewer. Be sure you illustrate that you are familiar with the type of training and other offerings at the program and how your skills and needs match the experience offered. Explain what is special about you. Be intentional with every word you choose to use. To be more purposeful and effective in your letter, make sure you understand the reason why you are sharing certain information.

Building anticipation and immediately engaging the reader in a cover letter takes some thought and practice. But you cannot afford to make the reviewer work hard to figure out if they should interview you. You do not want them to think, "I don't get it—Why are they applying to my site? Nothing I'm reading here sounds relevant to the training we offer." Instead, by the end of reading your cover letter, you want the reviewer to be captivated and think, "I definitely need to meet or talk to this person!"

The most important question to answer in your cover letter is, "How do you envision our internship site meeting your training goals and interests?" This is both an invitation and a mandate to address site-specific issues and the training opportunities. You can only do this by writing a custom letter for each site.

Begin by providing a brief opening. State why you are writing, the slot or rotation you are seeking, and why the site is attractive to you. Then move on and delve right in to your skills and goals. Briefly identify one or two specific internship goals that align to the training. Highlight your skills through examples, and succinctly explain how your interests fit with the site's opportunities for training. To do this, think about what really interests you in the site, why you would be a great intern and then clearly explain that association. Be sure to mention specific projects, research or experiences you have had that correspond to the program's offerings. The following is an example that incorporates all the aforementioned suggestions.

> With excitement and great anticipation, I have watched the opportunities at your program grow since it became APA-accredited in 2016. I am energized by Dr. Smith's innovative work in childhood posttraumatic stress disorder (PTSD) because it strongly resonates with my theoretical approach and is one of my main professional passions. Spending two practicum years working in a battered women's shelter, I have developed a deep commitment to applying more effective single session interventions with this often-transient population. This month, I am completing the data analysis for my dissertation on PTSD among school-aged children of Latinas who have had short stays at shelters. These experiences motivate me to learn the newest evidence-based approaches with this particular demographic, which is an attractive hallmark of your program.

This writer packed a lot of helpful and alluring information into this short paragraph. It shows that he or she

- has done their research on the program;
- is up to date in the latest evidence-based PTSD treatments;
- has experience in, and reasons for, their interest in an area for which the program is well-known; and
- has done short-term therapy and wants to learn more.

It also explains the status of the writer's dissertation or doctoral project. Another possibility for the body of your cover letter is to point out any relevant paid work experience or certifications you hold that are germane.

For the closing of your cover letter, it is appropriate to end with a more assertive message that shows your interest in the opportunity, rather than the standard (translation: boring), "I look forward to hearing from you." One of the many potential ways to communicate the genuine enthusiasm we recommend you demonstrate throughout the process is by closing with something akin to the following:

> Given your faculty's unique contributions to advancing evidenced-based PTSD treatment strategies, I am thrilled by the prospect of interning at your site. The complementary training you offer in developing community partnerships further cements my deep

interest in working with you. After talking with several of your past interns about your hands-on mentoring approach, I welcome the chance for an interview to better assess how we might have a mutually rewarding training experience together. Sincerely, Your Name.

Between the last two examples above, a lot of helpful, attention-grabbing, specific information has been provided in comparatively few words that motivates the reviewer to want to learn more. Hopefully you can see how every word was used with intention and the reviewer can see explicit links between your practicum experience, research, and training goals, and several aspects of their program that correspond to your background and interests. It will take a few drafts to eliminate wordiness in your cover letter and distill it down to the most relevant aspects of your message. But it is much better to provide a short letter chocked full of great information than to fill two full pages with words that ultimately do not hook the reader and leave him or wanting to dig into your application to discover more about you.

Sometimes applicants appropriately use the cover letter to make the selection committee aware of any personal reason they may have for relocation. This is not required, but for example, if you are looking for an opportunity to tell the committee that you would really like to return to your hometown next year, then this may be the place to do it. Or, you may wish to let the committee know that you would seriously consider relocating (e.g., "I am looking forward to the possibility of moving to Honolulu") to help convey your interest in the site. This may be especially important for programs that are in less desirable locations. If you decide to briefly mention your reasons for relocation, be sure that you do so in a way that makes it clear that location is only one of many reasons that you are interested in a program. Otherwise, the selection committee may be left thinking that you are applying primarily because you want to live in that geographic area and not because the program is a good fit for your training goals.

Questions about personal disclosure throughout your application materials are common. People often wonder if they can disclose too much or if they should disclose any information that might be considered personal. The answers to these questions are very dependent on your level of comfort, the type of training environment you are seeking, and how personal information is couched. In general, as tempting as it may be to add a lot of personality, fun and flair to a cover letter through personal disclosures, most people appreciate a cover letter that is judicious and professional. Humor can be very subjective, especially in writing, so be sure that you ask others for a perception check before you include any attempts at levity. Think about the visual you are creating in a reader's mind by the words, examples, and tone you use. You are writing a short story about who you are as an emerging psychologist. From the start, you want to send the message that you are affable, ready to learn, and trainable and that you will fit in and enhance their culture. You do not want to be seen as odd or that you have unconventional outside interests that may impede your ability to be taken seriously. "Here's who I am and what I bring to the table" is the message you want to relay. The entire point of the cover letter is to outline the fit and generate enough interest for the site to invite you to interview.

"Selling" the Fit

If the cover letter is the only place in your application materials in which you are discussing your training goals and how you perceive that these goals fit the opportunities offered at the training site, then you need to go back and revise Essays 1 through 4! The cover letter should be an abstract of your entire application. It should be a brief statement of your training goals and the main focus should be on articulating the exact rotations, didactic seminars, philosophies, supervisors, and other site qualities that directly fit your interests. This is where training directors are going to look for this information. Do not make them guess what aspects of their program interest you. You have to be very explicit and sell yourself. Below are some strategies to help you suspend any tendency to be overly humble or underestimate yourself, and instead, take ownership of what you have to offer and what you want.

- *Use strong language.* If you think that this site is a unique or exceptional match, then say so. Convince the reader that training at his or her site would be ideal to help you achieve your specific training goals. This is not the place to let the reader connect the dots and try to draw the conclusions that you are trying to creatively lead them to. Be overt, clear, and direct.
- *List rotations/experiences.* Yes, this will mean that you will need to rewrite this statement, in part or whole, for each application. However, if the essays generally state your goals for training overall, then the cover letter may be the only document that you need to substantially revise for each site. It is a good idea to list the rotations and experiences that are of greatest interest. You are not committing to a specific training plan now, but you can make it clear that there are several exciting opportunities that match your interests, and you easily could be happy with a combination of the experiences offered at the site. Do not state that "everything at your site sounds great!" because that does not suggest a specific match and can sound disingenuous.
- *Be authentic.* Do not state a fit if there is not one. Remember, you are looking for not just a slot but the best fit. If you say you are interested in something that you are not, or if you exaggerate the level of your interest, you are doing a disservice not only to the site and the other applicants but also most certainly to yourself. It is interesting to note that many applicants report that they write their first cover letter to the site that they are most interested in, and then in descending order of interest thereafter. By application number 10 or so, many applicants realize that they are having a hard time writing a compelling fit argument in their cover letter and decide not to apply to some of these poorer-fit sites after all. This is good. If you do not see a fit, neither will the site!
- *Be enthusiastic!* You have been in the same graduate program for at least 3 (maybe 10?) years. This is a chance to go out into the world and establish your professional identity beyond the walls of your school. This is the beginning of everything that led you to pursue graduate training so many years ago. Sure, you may be tired now, distressed about your dissertation, and worried about obtaining an internship match. Yes, you may have questioned your career choice several times over the past 3 or more rigorous years of training. But now you are almost there, and your career is about to change forever. Remember how excited you were when you were admitted to graduate school and thought about a career as a practitioner, researcher, consultant, or teacher? Reclaim that enthusiasm, if only for a moment! And then write the letter.

SUMMARY Many applicants view the AAPI essays and the cover letter as major roadblocks to completing applications for internship. Indeed, the task of writing five stories about your personal and professional selves can be intimidating and even emotionally exhausting. Nevertheless, by clarifying your professional goals prior to starting the essays, you can connect those short stories into one longer, more powerful story, and you can increase the likelihood of communicating your fit with internship sites.

Once you have written a stellar and compelling set of essays and a cover letter that makes the reader beg to learn more about you, it is time to think about your supplementary materials and your approach to the interview process; these are discussed in the next two chapters of this workbook.

Sample Cover Letter

Dear Dr. X:

Thank you for reviewing my application to the predoctoral internship training program at the Community Behavioral Health Clinic (CBHC). I am a clinical psychology doctoral candidate in my fifth year at the University of [State]. I believe my interests and graduate training experiences make me an excellent candidate for your internship program. Included with this letter, please find the AAPI online application, graduate transcript, CV, and four letters of recommendation.

Consistent with the ideals of the scientist–practitioner model, I am committed to a career that combines and, thus, mutually enriches clinical practice, teaching, and clinically relevant research. Overall, I am extremely interested in the program at CBHC because it would allow me to further develop as a versatile and competent clinician, as well as a productive researcher. Moreover, I am drawn to your program's dual emphasis on evidence-based practice and applied research to inform the development and implementation of future treatments. Based on your program materials, reputation, and the report of a current trainee, I believe that your program is ideally suited to my accomplishing my primary training goals. Each of these is outlined below.

First, I wish to continue to develop broad-based competencies in conducting assessment and therapy with populations that are diverse in terms of developmental stages, clinical presentations, and multicultural backgrounds and identities. As such, I am thrilled by the unparalleled opportunity afforded to each intern at CBHC to collaboratively develop an individual training program. My intention would be to take full advantage of this flexibility, first by advancing my emerging specialization in working with children, adolescents, and families across a variety of inpatient and outpatient rotations. Additionally, my clinical and research endeavors to date have taught me to appreciate the compelling utility of a developmental, lifespan psychopathology perspective. Accordingly, I am equally committed to further developing my intervention and assessment skills with adult populations. I am excited by your program's opportunities to gain general clinical training through a wide variety of adult rotations.

Second, I am excited by the unique opportunity CBHC would offer for me to balance a breadth of clinical experiences with more focused training in areas of emerging specialization. My clinical and research interests concentrate on adolescent anxiety and shared mechanisms of emotion dysregulation. For example, I am currently performing crisis evaluations with adolescents and parents participating in an NIMH-funded study of adolescent obsessive-compulsive disorder. I wish to continue to deepen and expand my assessment and intervention skills with high-risk populations. I would be thrilled by the opportunity to gain advanced training in the Assessment and Treatment of Adolescent Anxiety Disorders Program, as well as in the psychiatric emergency room of the Diagnostic Evaluation Center.

Third, and relatedly, given my deep commitment to the integration of science and practice in my career, I wish to gain additional research training and experiences on internship and beyond. I will have defended my dissertation project in advance of my internship year and, as such, I would be interested in pursuing additional, independent research opportunities with several of your research preceptors. In particular, I would be excited to continue my research in the area of adolescent anxiety under the mentorship of Dr. [Name]. I believe that the experience of conducting clinical research at CBHC would be integral in preparing me for a practice and research-oriented career within an urban, academic medical center.

Fourth, to more effectively address a full spectrum of clinical presentations, I wish to enhance my solid grounding in CBT case formulation and intervention with continued exposure to empirically supported treatments. Accordingly, the CBHC program's explicit commitment to the application of evidence-based practice is an obvious draw. As well, I seek continued supervision in the application of integrated theoretical models of psychotherapy to meet the unique needs and preferences of each individual client. I am excited by your program's opportunities to receive supervision in several therapeutic modalities and theoretical orientations, including CBT, DBT, and IPT approaches.

Finally, and on a more personal level, my partner and I are hoping to return to Honolulu for internship. I am from Hawaii and several of my immediate family members and friends still reside there. Training at CBHC would allow me to benefit from the phenomenal training opportunities at your site while enabling me to return to the region of the country where I hope to establish myself professionally.

Thank you again for considering my application. Should you have any questions, please do not hesitate to contact me by phone. I look forward to hearing from you.

Best regards,

Your Name

4 CURRICULUM VITAE AND LETTERS OF RECOMMENDATION

You have calculated your hours, entered information into your Association of Psychology Postdoctoral and Internship Centers (APPIC) Application for Psychology Internships (AAPI), and written thoughtful essays and a cover letter that carefully describes your training and career goals. The next steps in the application process are to assemble or update your curriculum vitae (CV) and to request letters of recommendation.

Ultimately, the manner in which you prepare your CV will be based on your own professional style and personal preferences. Likewise, you should give some serious thought to whom you ask to write letters of recommendation, why they are the best choices, and how you can provide them with helpful information to write an extraordinary letter on your behalf. To help you prepare for these components of your application, this chapter offers some guidance on the underlying purpose of each and the most effective strategies to represent your best authentic self. Remembering that your application materials will be reviewed in their entirety and your CV and recommendations will provide more context pertaining to how you are emerging as a professional, you will want all your documents to fit together as a cohesive package. Recognize that these additional pieces of information are opportunities to strengthen your application. They should not be overly repetitive but instead should add depth, detail, and validation that compellingly sells you as an interesting and qualified internship applicant.

Although there is no "one best way" to construct a CV, there are some universally accepted frameworks and certain categories of information nuanced for psychology that everyone expects to see on your CV to help them evaluate your background and the fit. You can find a lot of advice on the Internet, in business publications, and elsewhere about how to write a terrific CV. Some people may even use fee-for-service

http://dx.doi.org/10.1037/0000102-004
Internships in Psychology: The APAGS Workbook for Writing Successful Applications and Finding the Right Fit, Fourth Edition, by C. Williams-Nickelson, M. J. Prinstein, and W. G. Keilin

résumé writing assistance, although we suggest you save your money for traveling to interviews or a well-deserved celebratory meal after you are matched. Whatever you do, resist any temptation to use quirky tactics to stand out on a professional document.

YOUR CURRICULUM VITAE

Internship sites expect that you will submit a CV with your application and not a résumé. A résumé is a one- to two-page snapshot of you and your qualifications for a particular job. With limitations in length, a résumé only reveals a high-level view of your education, work experience, research, publications, volunteerism, and awards. A résumé typically starts with a statement of goals, purpose, or objectives, followed by a list of specific job skills, tangible and measurable accomplishments in your work roles, and other notable achievements that show you meet the requirements and can perform the necessary work in a certain role.

Curriculum vitae is Latin for the "course of [one's] life." A CV is unlimited in length and is an evolving document that chronicles your professional development and career. It includes all the information covered on a résumé in greater depth and detail but generally does not include a statement of your goals and objectives. More specifically, a CV records more descriptive information about your skills, expertise, areas of specialty training, or focus; work experience and range of related responsibilities; accomplishments and outcomes related to your unique contributions to projects; and information that reflects intangibles, such as your desire to succeed and ability to lead. It is a comprehensive record of your progression as a professional. At this stage of your professional development, your CV is likely to be a five- to 10-page document but will vary based on your life situation.

Write your CV with your audience in mind. Think about who you are speaking to and what they want and need to know about your background. Obviously, in this case, your audience includes practitioner psychologists who are internship training directors and faculty. Therefore, emphasizing your clinical experiences and the skills and competencies you are developing with different populations in various environments is essential. It is also important to include your research; practicum training; provision of supervision; teaching experience, with the level of responsibility for the course; peer reviewed and professional development publications (in separate categories); leadership activities; volunteer work; professional memberships; awards; other languages spoken and written, along with fluency level; and other areas of involvement that contribute to your ability to be a great intern.

The structure and style of your CV can be as important as the content. Avoid distracting the reader with a strange layout, unreadable fonts, or so many mistakes that they cannot concentrate on the content or make sense of your developmental trajectory. Similarly, as members of a profession with intelligent, contemplative, and scientifically minded people, we tend to be verbose, often when it is not necessary or particularly effective. The more obscure words we use to describe and explain things, the more we think people will better understand what we are trying to communicate, and the more scholarly we feel. But the opposite is true when it comes to CVs. We can learn a lot from the public relations and marketing professions that will help us become more effective communicators when time and space are limited. Your CV will be more effortlessly absorbed if you are economical with your use of words; consistent with your style, grammar, and tense; and if you use an active voice. A sloppy CV may be interpreted as indicative of a careless intern.

Years ago, people tended to reveal a lot of personal information on their CVs, including photographs. You might even find some bad advice on reputable online sites about branding your CV in these outdated ways as a means to stand out. However, this type of personalization is rarely viewed positively in the field of psychology. We strongly recommend that you not include a picture, your date of birth, the number of children you have, your height and weight, your astrological sign, or similar items. These inclusions are mostly irrelevant information and are likely to give the impression of padding your CV with superfluous material so your background appears more robust. More commonly seen are CVs that list classes taken, class presentations, published abstracts, names of conferences or workshops attended, and so forth.

Most sites will ask for a transcript that already documents your coursework. Nearly every graduate student delivers many class presentations as a routine part of the curriculum, and you are therefore expected to be practiced in this area. These are not unique accomplishments or activities that bolster your CV. Perhaps your intent in adding a list of conferences that you attended is to demonstrate that you go above and beyond to learn more than your program offers and to be involved in organized psychology. This is great! Think of how you can represent those behaviors and attitudes more naturally throughout your application materials rather than using extraneous lists. On the other hand, if you attended a conference or workshop for which you had a unique role or gained a special skill that is relevant to the internship sites you are applying to, it would be perfectly acceptable to include that information in context.

Other common but questionable text includes, for example, information about where you attended high school, that you were the captain of your college football team, or that you won a beauty contest. Although some training directors may be interested in hearing about these aspects of your life, we think that it is better to save this personal information for a conversation rather than to categorize these as academic achievements on your CV.

Remember that it is not the length of your CV that matters most. It is the quality, significance, and clarity of the information provided for the purpose of identifying a fit. The desire to create a lengthy CV usually originates from a concern that one has too few accomplishments or may be evaluated as underqualified. To reiterate, you are applying for a training position. You are not expected to enter internship as a seasoned, fully competent, independent practitioner. You need to demonstrate that you are trainable and that there are distinct areas in which more training will make you a better clinician. This means that you are not expected to have an extensive history of accomplishments. If the director of clinical training in your graduate program says that you are ready to apply for internship, then you probably are!

It is worth mentioning that for some counseling or more psychodynamically oriented internships, training directors might have a greater interest in learning about who you are as a person outside of psychology as they evaluate the fit between what you are seeking and the training experience they offer. As such, if you wish to include a "hobbies and interests" section on your CV, we recommend a brief insert at the end of your CV that includes some of this personal, yet appropriate, information. Here's an example.

> Hobbies/Interests: Avid weekend gardener, certified yoga instructor and reflexologist, high school swim coach, equestrian champion, skydiver, mountaineer, deep sea fisherperson, longboard surfer, classical opera singer.

Because your CV is a tool to inform and persuade, it should be written in a captivating and accurate manner. Although your CV is not a creative essay, it is a reflection of who you are and it should tell a story about the experiences that have shaped your professional identity. Therefore, you want to be sure that the reader is not distracted by typos, misspellings, an illogical flow, or unusual fonts and formatting. As with everything else, give your CV to others to review. An error-free CV that includes fluid and easy to understand transitions will paint a coherent picture of you as a growing professional, make a great impression, and improve your overall application.

Constructing Your CV

Weaving your achievements throughout your CV tells a consistent story about your strengths and specific ways you contribute to enriching your training environment. Yet many people often struggle with identifying and describing their achievements well. Below are some prompts to help you think about how you might describe some of your achievements.

1. What have you done over and above expectations?
2. When did you save the day? How did you do it and what were the circumstances?
3. Where have you demonstrated flexibility, and why was it important in that situation?
4. Where have you shown creative thinking or innovation and what impact did it have?
5. How have you demonstrated your commitment to the profession?
6. What projects or extra activities have you been involved in, and what was your contribution to the outcome?
7. What legacy have you left behind in your program?
8. What problems have you solved?
9. What did the department/practicum site/research lab look like when you left compared with when you started, and what part did you play in that?
10. What will your program miss the most about you when you leave for internship and graduate?

The following checklist list offers best practices and overarching strategies that will help you prepare to write a CV that is effective in presenting your experiences and skills in a professional manner.

- Understand the different purposes and formats of a résumé and a CV, and be sure to submit a CV with your internship application.
- Edit several drafts of your CV over time to make it clearer, more concise, and increasingly polished before you submit it to internship sites. As an evolving document, your CV is endlessly perfectible, but you are not required to submit a perfect document.

- Ask trusted faculty members to review your CV and provide you with feedback about its content and organization.
- Do not use acronyms but feel free to use commonly understood psychology terms, as needed, to be succinct. Discipline-specific language is the shortest, clearest, and most suitable way to communicate within one's field.
- Use your CV to inform and persuade but do not try to instruct.
- Anticipate what readers want and need to know about you, and place information in a logical and progressive format.
- Identify the primary audience for your CV. For example, consider the type of site to which you are applying (e.g., counseling center, Veterans Affairs, medical center). How much does your audience know about your experiences (i.e., your program, your practica, your work experience, your professional involvement)? What questions can you anticipate from your audience and address in your CV? Have you omitted any significant information that the audience needs?
- Be specific and precise, but recognize that, depending on experience, education, mind-sets, and conceptual frameworks, every CV reader will react differently to the same words on a page, and you will not have complete control over interpretation.
- Present the facts without distortion. Do not overinflate your achievements or mislead the reader.
- Accurately present your skills by describing what you have done and what you do. Avoid using broad adjectives and pretentious, obscure, and esoteric language. For example, the words *responsible*, *dependable*, and *committed* are too vague. Describe how you have been responsible. Offer information that will help the reader see that you are dependable. Describe projects or activities you have been involved with and seen through to the end to demonstrate commitment.
- Use fewer words when possible to convey the same meaning; complete sentences are not necessary.
- Only use lists when additional context is not necessary, when they boost your qualifications, and when the purpose is obvious.
- Keep any lists used consistent in grammatical form (all verbs, or all nouns or noun forms, or all complete sentences).
- Use an active voice as much as possible. Use present and past tenses appropriately.
- Vary word choice (find synonyms for overused words like *provide*) and keep it simple (e.g., *use* is better than *utilize*).
- Use topic headings to increase organization and ease of readability and avoid excessive subheadings.
- Do not offer information just because you have it. Evaluate the purpose of all the information you include.
- Limit personal information that might lead to assumptions about your life. Think about your goal in providing any personal disclosures. Do not include a picture.
- Think of your CV as your written portrait. The physical appearance, or format, of your CV is important—it affirms your ability to communicate and overall professionalism.

Organizing Your CV

The information on your CV should be organized into logical groupings. The following is an outline and discussion of the major areas of the CV in the order that most would expect.

1. Name, Address, Telephone and Fax Number(s) With Area Code, and E-mail Address
   - Position this information at the top of the first page.
   - Place last name and page number at the top or bottom of every additional page.
   - Use a permanent address and telephone number where you are sure mail and messages can be received and will be delivered to you; if applicable, list a daytime and an evening number.
2. Education
   - List the entries in reverse chronological order (beginning with most recent, or highest degree attained).
   - List the name, location (city, state), degree earned, graduation date, major(s), cumulative GPAs (optional), and GPAs in major (optional) for each university and degree.
   - List honors, scholarships, and awards; you may choose to list these with each institution or under a separate category.
   - Do not include high school, as it is generally not necessary.
   - Include information about all undergraduate and graduate programs that you attended, even if some are in fields that are unrelated to psychology and even if your attendance did not result in the attainment of a degree.
3. Employment (if applicable)
   - List entries in reverse chronological order, starting with the most recent job.
   - Include the businesses' name, department (if appropriate), and the city and state. You may also choose to list your immediate supervisor's name, if desired.
   - Do not report salary information.
   - List the last position or job title you held. If you held more than one position or title at the same job site, list those consecutively with the dates those positions were held. Alternatively, if you had distinct responsibilities associated with each position that you would like to distinguish, list the job position with the responsibilities below, followed by the other job position/title with the related responsibilities below.
   - List your dates of employment from month/year to month/year.
   - Include a narrative or bullet points that describe your specific duties, including workload, type of work, level of responsibility, supervision provided to others, programs developed or administered, special projects, achievements, promotions, positions held that led to current position, and any budgetary responsibilities (use active voice and avoid vague adjectives). It is often helpful to include bullet points with measurable achievements to show your unique contributions to the business.
   - Include work awards and commendations.
   - Do not include your reason for leaving the position.

Here is an example of how you might present your employment information:

PacifiCare, Inc. October 2017–Present
Somewhere North, CA *Supervisor:* Martin Evil, MBA

Position: Claims Reviewer and Authorizer

Responsibilities: Provide consultation to physicians in developing insurance-approved treatment plans; authorize laboratory work and medical testing based on insurer's benefit plan and medical need; complete quarterly cost–benefit analyses; and specialize in administration of behavioral health services.

4. Volunteer or Service Work
   - Format this section similar to the employment section with name, mailing address, area code and telephone number, supervisor or volunteer coordinator, and dates of service.
   - Include an official title, if applicable.
   - Report responsibilities.
5. Practicum or Psychotherapy Experience
   - Format this section similar to the employment and volunteer sections.
   - Include the names of all supervisors.
   - Specify type of services, population served, special treatment protocol and interventions used, amount of testing, consultation, multidisciplinary team work, average time spent weekly or monthly at the site, range of presenting problems, psychotropic medication management, and other services provided.

Here is an example of how to present your practicum or psychotherapy experience:

Friendly Medical Center September 2017–Present
Department of Behavioral Medicine *Supervisor:* Sandy Stressfree, PhD
Merryville, AZ

Responsibilities: Provide health psychology services to a range of patients with cognitive impairment, high blood pressure, chronic pain, and depression; complete neuropsychological assessments; provide individual and group therapy to patients and their family members; work as part of an interdisciplinary team with psychiatrists, physicians, nurses, social workers, and rehabilitation therapists in the urology, cardiac, surgical recovery, and orthopedic departments; use hypnotherapy and cognitive behavior therapy interventions; conduct standardized smoking cessation programs; and participate in grand rounds.

Hours: approximately 20 hours per week.

6. Provision of Clinical Supervision (if applicable)
   - This may be part of a class in supervision.
   - Include the name of the licensed supervisor ultimately responsible for the clients and their student therapists that you supervise.
   - Describe your supervisory experience and style.
   - Describe the type of supervision offered (e.g., live, group, individual, videotaped, audiotaped).

- List supervisee characteristics (e.g., provided supervision to social workers, master's counseling students; primarily supervised couples therapy cases).

7. Professional Affiliations and Leadership Roles
   - List all memberships in professional associations.
   - List level of membership (e.g., affiliate, student, associate, full), and make sure you are documenting your membership type correctly.
   - Indicate membership duration.
   - Describe the professional organization if it is not commonly known.
   - List any offices, roles, or projects associated with professional organization membership or involvement.
   - List special committee memberships (e.g., advisory board, steering committee, school senate).

8. Awards and Scholarships
   - List the name of the award or scholarship, who nominated, who bestowed, type of award or scholarship, and date conferred. (There are very few universally recognized and understood awards and scholarships, so you need to describe what you won and why you won it.)
   - Indicate dollar amounts for awards or scholarships if they are substantial or provide important information.
   - Do not include awards that are not meaningful (e.g., "listed in the *Who's Who Among Psychology Graduate Students*").

9. Licensure
   - Include any licenses you hold, the name of the licensing board, the date the license was obtained, and your license number.

10. Teaching Experience
    - List the name of university, department, city/state, dates of teaching, and supervisor(s) names in a format similar to the employment listings.
    - Indicate the name and level of the course(s) you taught and the number of times each course was taught at each institution.
    - The responsibilities of teaching assistants vary widely. It is helpful to include your specific role as a teaching assistant. Did you develop the entire syllabus and have full responsibility for developing lectures, giving and grading student assignments and examinations, and assigning final grades? Was your role to run the lab and answer questions after lectures from a professor? Did you grade papers and exams only?

11. Research
    - List your research projects as well as your dissertation research.
    - Include details about the nature of your research involvement. (Do you work directly with participants, analyze data, train research assistants to administer certain assessments?)
    - Include the names of your research supervisor(s), dissertation chair, and purpose of the research (i.e., research assistant, significant class project).

12. Grants
    - List the title of the project, name of the funding agency, and dates of the funding.
    - List your role on the grant (Principal Investigator, Co-Principal Investigator, Co-Investigator, Consultant).
    - Include the dollar amount of the grant (optional).

13. Professional Presentations
    - List presentations at professional conferences and workshops.
    - Use the most recent American Psychological Association (APA) Style guidelines for citing presentations.
14. Publications
    - List any publications and manuscripts in print, in press, under review, and (perhaps) in preparation.
    - Use the most recent APA Style guidelines for citing publications.
    - List only peer-reviewed articles and professional publications, such as book chapters.
15. Other sections (if applicable)
    - List conferences attended only if you have a specific reason (e.g., to document specialty training) for including this information (and make that reason clear to the reviewer).
    - List special courses only if you have a specific reason (e.g., to document unique certification of skills) for including this information. Be sure to make the reason clear. Your internship site will have a copy of your transcripts.
16. References
    - Be sure to check with references before providing their names and contact information to others and try to alert them of any potential calls ahead of time.
    - Give your references your CV and other information to make it easy for them to highlight your outstanding accomplishments.

LETTERS OF RECOMMENDATION

In recent years, some have questioned the relative importance of recommendation letters in the internship application process. Are they just a formality to make sure everyone has three references in their file? What kind of weight do they carry in the site's decision-making process? Make no mistake, recommendation letters are an extremely important part of your application materials and you should not underestimate their ability to tip a ranking decision one way or the other. In fact, some training directors have expressed that after they verify that an applicant has met the minimum qualifications for their internship and has written a cover letter and essay that are compatible with the training offered, they use the recommendation letters to determine whom they will invite for an interview.

Recommendation letters serve several purposes. Not only do they attest to your internship readiness but they also provide information about how you are viewed by others. They speak to your character traits, your professionalism, and your normalcy. They are also an opportunity for your supervisors to discuss superior skills you possess and other desirable attributes, such as problem solving, working collaboratively with a team, case conceptualization, client relationships, leadership, ability to cooperate and get along with others in an academic and social context, ambition, drive, and ethics. Training directors often look for evidence of other attractive traits in recommendations indicating that the applicant is generally a good, kind, accepting, supportive, and hard-working contributor.

Another important objective of recommendation letters is to offer ideas for areas of focus for your internship training. Yes, this means your weaknesses. If a site cannot identify how they can help further your training and assist you in developing new skills, they may not see that they have very much to offer you. Understanding your areas for growth from the perspective of a recent or current supervisor is useful. It demonstrates that you are trainable, and it generates excitement among internship staff that they could have the opportunity to contribute to your professional growth.

Your references will complete a Standardized Reference Form (SRF) through AAPI Online. References are asked to answer the four main questions below, primarily in a narrative format.

1. How they know you and for how long.
2. Activities you have performed under their guidance and supervision.
3. Your areas of clinical interest and career aspirations, and your current path of professional development.
4. Your specific competencies and growth areas.

Although this is a standard form that asks for the same information and poses the same questions to every reference, open-ended questions still provide plenty of flexibility for your references to address the areas suggested in this section. References are asked to be brief in their responses and their letters may not exceed two pages in length. Addressing competencies with which your reference is familiar is noted as highly desirable in the areas of research, ethical and legal standards, individual and cultural diversity, professional values and attitudes, communication and interpersonal skills, assessment, intervention, supervision, consultation and interprofessional/interdisciplinary skills.

Most applicants can secure positive letters of recommendation that attest to clinical competence and internship readiness. This is the baseline expectation. However, what sets your recommendations apart is evidence of the following:

1. You are genuinely liked and respected by your peers, faculty, and supervisors.
2. You consistently demonstrate professionalism.
3. You are collegial, respectful and can work well with others, including peers, supervisors, and subordinates.
4. You are committed to learning and are receptive to feedback; even though you may enter the internship with impressive skills, you are interested in expanding those skills and believe others have valuable knowledge to share with you.
5. You are responsible, responsive, sensible, and hardworking, and you complete high-quality work.
6. You are a leader but you also know when it is important to follow the direction of others.
7. You are invested in the profession and will represent the profession well.
8. You are *normal*. Others gravitate toward you, not away from you. Sites want to know what kind of a person you are because they will be spending a lot of time with you over the next year.

How do you get someone to write a recommendation that validates and adds perspective to what you discussed in your cover letter and that addresses the key questions on the SRF? First and foremost, keep in mind that your faculty and supervisors want you to be successful in your internship search. They want to help you evaluate your strengths and weaknesses and assist you in the development of meaningful training goals, if you are amenable to their input. They know that part of their role as a supervisor is to write internship recommendations for their students. They will gladly provide a reference, but they need you to do the brunt of the work through self-evaluation and drafting, revising, and effectively articulating your goals. You can make your reference's recommendation writing a little easier if you:

- Identify references early.
- Meet with your references periodically to allow them to get to know you over time.
- Provide a copy of your cover letter, CV, essays, and goals for internship to review and discuss together.
- Consider providing a bulleted reference sheet to help your supervisors formulate what they want to say in their recommendations. This reference sheet might include notes about your work together and it can serve to remind them of your specific competencies, accomplishments, and areas for growth (see example in Exhibit 4.1)

As you think about whom you would like to approach about writing a recommendation letter, keep in mind that your goal is to obtain recommendations that offer the most accurate and positive description of your skills, accomplishments, and personal demeanor. Always ask potential references some version of the question, "Do you think you know me well enough to write a *strong* letter of support for me?" If that individual answers yes without hesitation, you can assume that his or her letter will be helpful. If that person expresses any reservations, you should ask someone else. Indeed, training directors have all too frequently commented that they are shocked by the lack of substance in some of the recommendation letters they receive, as well as some letters that nearly say, "I do not recommend this student for internship at this time." It seems odd and counterintuitive (Why would a supervisor write a recommendation that is not flattering?), but disconnects occur between applicants and their supervisors and programs, and these types of letters can ensure you are not ranked.

Applicants often have many questions about who makes the best references. These questions include, Is it okay to have two of my supervisors from the same practicum site write letters? Does this make it seem like my other practicum supervisors cannot write strong letters? What if all my letters are from junior faculty? Will it increase my chances of being ranked high if I have famous psychologists write my letters?

Our advice is that you try not to overthink the rank, tenure, perceived status, or other characteristics and accomplishments of your references. Your main focus should be on asking licensed psychologists who know you and your clinical work very well. Usually, the high-profile psychologist letters do not impress internship sites, unless these psychologists can speak in-depth about your clinical and personal skills. If you have the choice between sending a weak letter from someone whom you believe to be a "famous" psychologist versus a very strong letter from a junior faculty member who has supervised your work closely and over time, we recommend that you ask the junior faculty member to write the letter.

Some people also question whether it is advisable to solicit a letter of recommendation from a nonpsychologist (e.g., a physician, psychiatrist, social worker). Although such professionals may be able to comment on your ability to work in a multidisciplinary setting, it is less likely that they will be able to comment on the types of skills

Exhibit 4.1. *Sample Request for Recommendation Letter*

Reference/letter writer:	Chris Pratt, PhD
Applicant name:	Jennifer Lawrence
Supervision provided by Reference:	9/2016–8/2017: Postpartum Depression Practicum 6/2018–Present: Advanced Practicum
Internship sites I am applying to:	1. Veterans Affairs Medical Center, Washington, DC 2. Hollywood Medical Center, Psychiatry Dept., CA 3. Mission Impossible Hospital, Dept. of Behavioral Science, MS 4. Cocktail Consortium, NV 5. Far Away School of Medicine/Psychiatry, NY 6. Magnolia Consortium, TX 7. Charleston Health Sciences Center, SC
Please highlight as you deem appropriate:	1. My level of enthusiasm and motivation. 2. Ability to connect with clients and create a therapeutic alliance. 3. My clinical skills, including case conceptualization, treatment planning, and treatment implementation. 4. Interest in learning a treatment modality that incorporates my research interests. 5. My ability to work with a patient with a trauma history. *I'm really interested in continuing to work with trauma on internship. All of the sites I'm applying to have major rotations that involve PTSD treatment, and you are the only supervisor who is in a position to comment on my ability to work with clients who have a history of trauma.* 6. My ability to balance acceptance and change strategies with my clients. *I'm thinking about the case of the comorbid client we worked on together as a good example of this.* 7. My professionalism, understanding of ethics, cultural competence, and ability to work in an interdisciplinary context. *A relevant example might be the case you supervised where I worked with law enforcement, protective services, and school administration.*
See attached for:	1. CV 2. Draft internship cover letter and essays 3. Past practicum evaluation

and competencies that are expected of doctoral-level psychologists; therefore, it may be better to obtain letters exclusively from psychologists. On the other hand, if a non-psychologist knows you well and fully understands the range of professional capabilities that should be addressed in a letter of recommendation for psychology internships, this person may be in an excellent position to be one of your recommenders.

And under no circumstances should you ever ask for a letter from your therapist! Your therapist cannot speak to your clinical skills, although he or she can talk about you in clinical terms. Similarly, letters from individuals with whom your relationship is primarily personal rather than professional, or from individuals who cannot speak directly to your strengths and weaknesses as a psychologist-in-training, should be avoided.

It is never too early to begin cultivating relationships with potential references. Make appointments to talk with your advisor, supervisors, and other faculty members whom you might ask to write letters. Provide them with a copy of your CV. Discuss your research ideas. Talk about your practica experiences and what you have learned about yourself through the successes you have had and the mistakes you have made. Share information about your previous jobs, volunteer work, and leadership activities. How have they influenced your clinical work and perspectives on culture? Most important, talk about your goals for training while on internship. Give these psychologists enough perspective that will help them form an accurate and comprehensive opinion of you so that they will have the necessary background to write a strong recommendation when the time comes.

Face your weaknesses head-on and introduce the topic of your growth areas with your potential references whenever possible. It is much better to know what your references will say about your weaknesses and have input into how they characterize them, than to wonder and even worry about what they might say and how you will respond in interviews to questions about your limitations. Everyone has room for improvement. If your references can talk about your ability to be introspective about your weaknesses and the steps you have already taken to address them, it speaks volumes about your ability and willingness to receive and incorporate feedback, as well as your commitment to continuously improving.

What helps to create a powerful recommendation letter?

1. *Specific information, skills and examples.* Patterns and illustrations of your work can be used to highlight your strengths and shape the reviewer's mental image of you.
2. *Context of how the writer knows you.* It is ideal if your reference can discuss where and how they have worked with you across a variety of settings, so the reviewer can conclude how representative and consistent the writer's experience is with you.
3. *Show that the writer knows you personally.* Interactions and observations that are unique to this relationship are more credible than information that could be easily gathered from the CV you have submitted.
4. *Provides specific examples of what you have done especially well.* If, for instance, you wrote a brilliant case study, your reference could discuss the reasons it stood out. The reference could also comment on any outstanding work in an area of focus for a certain internship site and describe how the internship relates to your goals or areas where you should stretch yourself.
5. *Discuss why you would be a strong candidate for a specific type of internship.* For example, how do you exemplify the personal qualities or selection criteria specified by the internship?
6. *Qualifications.* Commenting on concrete abilities provides specific links between your past performance and what is expected at the internship site.
7. *Placing you in a larger context.* This can include comparisons to others who have succeeded at the same site or in similar environments. Quantitative remarks and percentages may be useful, such as "John is among the top 5% of

students in my 20 years of teaching." The strongest comparisons have the widest reach. For instance, "Tiffany is among the best students in my 15 years of supervising" is stronger than "Tiffany is the best in this year's class." (Although the latter is still impressive.)

8. *Drawing on the remarks of colleagues.* This is used as supporting evidence or for acknowledging distinct talents. For example, "My colleagues and I have often remarked about Jennifer's keen ability to . . ." Recommendations from supervisors may also draw on the comments from other practicum staff who may have worked more closely with you but may not be licensed psychologists who provided direct supervision. A statement such as, "The nursing and administrative staff often remarked how much they appreciated Jillian's availability for impromptu consultations."

Although less compelling recommendations may not result in a failure to match, they can hurt you and your chances of matching to one of your top choices. The first question in the instance of a weak letter is, "What are they not telling me or purposely withholding about this student?" Less effective letters are

- too short and fail to provide specific examples of the general characteristics your reference mentions (e.g., "Suzie is a great therapist with children" does not say much);
- generic or obviously reused from another letter for another purpose, without regard to the type of site to which you are applying;
- merely a summary of information available elsewhere in your application;
- focused too much on the context (e.g., descriptions of the practicum or the approaches used and not sufficiently focused on you and how you executed those approaches);
- filled with unsupported praise, such as having kind words that do not set you apart (e.g., "Sally is an excellent practicum student" without substantiation is incomplete at best); and
- inclusive of only light praise—it is not very valuable to say that a student did what was expected (completed therapy notes after each session) or that point to qualities (punctuality, interest, and attendance) that are not relevant to the internship, that sound tepid, or suggest indifference.

Once you have identified your references and you are sure they are willing and prepared to write you an excellent reference, you must enter their information on the AAPI Online through the Applicant Portal. This will trigger the system to generate electronic requests for your references to complete the SRF mentioned earlier. These references will upload their SRF directly into the AAPI Online. It is then up to you to attach the SRF's to your applications. You have the option of asking as many references as you wish to complete a SRF. However, you may only submit three references to each site. Although you do not have access to the content in the SRF, you may attach it to as many or as few applications as you would like. Therefore, you have the ability to decide which SRFs are submitted to each internship site.

Why might you want more than three SRFs available for your use? Different references will know you and your work in different contexts. Depending on the type of sites to which you are applying, you may choose to have references who will be able to comment on your skills and training needs that are especially compatible with a particular type of training environment. For instance, you might be applying to medical centers with a focus on traumatic brain injury (TBI) and that have a research component. You might also be applying to clinics that provide out-patient rehabilitation services for a wide variety of clients, including but not limited to TBI clients. One reference might be an excellent reference for the medical centers that also emphasize research, and another reference might make a better case for your fit within a clinic setting. Therefore, you may decide to have a pool of five SRFs to choose from when submitting your maximum of three references to each internship site. Generally, though, most applicants will find that the same three SRFs are relevant to all the sites to which they are applying. Finally, if you are getting anxious that a reference who agreed to complete an SRF for you is falling behind and may not get it done in time, you have the option of asking as many additional references as you wish to help. This is uncommon, but it can provide a safety net in case you are worried that you will not have the requisite three SRFs for all sites.

ADDITIONAL SITE-SPECIFIC MATERIALS

Every so often, a site may ask you to include a work sample, such as a testing report or case summary, to supplement your application. If this happens to you, talk with your director of clinical training to determine which work sample should be included and how it should be presented to conceal the identity of the client, if relevant. After you obtain the work sample, you will need to convert it into an electronic format (usually by scanning the document) and upload it to the AAPI Online service as an attachment under "Supplementary Materials." It will then be submitted with your application to that program. Testing reports and case summaries are the only supplemental materials that programs are permitted to require, with a maximum of two. For instance, programs can ask for two testing reports or two summaries or one of each, but no more than two in total. Any other specific or unique information requested by a program can be addressed in the cover letter.

SUMMARY

The materials discussed in this chapter include a CV, recommendation letters, and any idiosyncratic materials that are site specific. Together, these materials provide a comprehensive review of your experience, illustrate your interests and how they have formed over time, and attest to your professionalism and perhaps also to some of your personal characteristics. At this point in the process, you can catch your breath. You have accomplished a lot! Give yourself a well-deserved pat on the back and find a way to celebrate. Then, take some time to rest. It is now the sites' turn to start reading through applications and deciding whom to invite for interviews. In only a few weeks, you should start hearing from sites to schedule interviews, which is the next major stage of the process and the subject of the next chapter.

5 THE INTERVIEW

Submitting your application materials is an accomplishment worthy of celebration and much relief. This milestone also begins a sometimes agonizing waiting period that ends once you receive your first decision notification regarding interviews. Sites vary considerably in the proportion of applicants they invite for an interview. Although some sites invite all applicants for a visit, you can expect that most sites will extend invitations to five to 10 applicants for every available internship slot. This chapter covers the basic information needed to successfully manage the interview process.

SCHEDULING INTERVIEWS

Over the years, it seems the timeline for scheduling interviews, and for interviews themselves, have moved up a bit. Although it used to be unheard of for interviews to take place in the month of December, it is now quite customary for early interviews (as early as December 1!) to occur and last throughout the month of January. In addition, many sites have begun notifying applicants with interview invitations in mid-November, sometimes just a few days or couple of weeks after most application deadlines. This is not necessarily great news for applicants. In addition to the absence of a needed reprieve from the rigorous application process, it also creates a bit of competition between sites trying to secure their top applicants for preferred interview days. This is worth addressing briefly here, as your negotiation skills may be tested early in the process.

Note that some sites allow you to select the date of your visit from many choices, whereas others may have only one or two dates to interview all invited applicants. Scheduling interviews thus can be a logistical challenge, particularly if you are fortunate enough to secure many interviews and if you are planning to visit sites around the country. (Note: National data indicate that the average number of interviews applicants

http://dx.doi.org/10.1037/0000102-005
Internships in Psychology: The APAGS Workbook for Writing Successful Applications and Finding the Right Fit, Fourth Edition, by C. Williams-Nickelson, M. J. Prinstein, and W. G. Keilin
Copyright © 2019 by the American Psychological Association. All rights reserved.

receive is between six and seven, and prediction analyses indicate that the likelihood of matching is remarkably high once this number of interviews has been secured.)

Internship sites may contact you to schedule an interview by mail, e-mail, or phone, and when they do, an overworked administrative assistant may hope to get quick answers from you to a variety of questions about your interview. Thus, it behooves you to carry a hard copy cheat sheet or calendar (there's no time to log into your computer when you get these calls!) of your ideal interview schedule to be prepared. Many sites will have listed their probable interview dates on their websites before your first notification, allowing you to draft a tentative plan for when you hope to be in each city and thus ready to respond to quick requests about your preferred interview slots. Ideally you will dedicate at least one full day of travel between any two interviews (note that this is the time period most fraught with travel delays/canceled flights, and you also will need rest between these long interview days!), and you will find out about interviews far enough in advance to secure the cheapest travel arrangements possible.

Inevitably, students face one of several dilemmas, however. A few suggestions are offered next.

Possible Dilemmas

Dilemma 1. You are unable to commit to Site A until you learn whether you will receive an interview at Site B.

Solution. Association of Psychology Postdoctoral and Internship Centers (APPIC) member sites must list in the *APPIC Directory Online* the date by which they will notify all applicants as to whether they are still being considered and will be invited for an interview. APPIC also has suggested that all sites notify applicants of their interview decisions by December 15. Yet, it is sometimes necessary and permissible to call an internship site prior to December 15 to ask whether you have been invited for an interview there so that you can coordinate travel plans. This is OK to try, but remember to be very nice to administrative assistants! They're trying as hard as they can, and they tell the faculty *everything!*

Dilemma 2. You got many more interviews than you expected, and you would rather not attend the ones at the bottom of your list.

Solution. There are many reasons why you should not decline an interview invitation. First, remember that the selection committee spent hours reviewing applications and carefully selected you. Rejecting an invitation means you have wasted their time, which may not be how you want to be remembered at this site. Second, applicants may not realize how often supervisors change locations, move to new sites, and continue to be involved in applicants' professional lives long after the internship match has ended. Thus, don't give away a chance to meet colleagues too quickly! Your opportunity to interview at a particular site may not lead to a mutual interest for your internship year, but it is highly likely your path, and the path of the people who may interview you will cross again. Third, note that many applicants' preferences regarding sites they have read about online change substantially once they have had an opportunity to interview. That site you think is your bottom choice may turn out to be your favorite!

Dilemma 3. You have a conflict between two interview invitations.

Solution. Most training directors recognize that there is competition among sites to secure their top candidates for desired interview dates, and thus, some rush to extend invitations. If you have a conflict between two different sites' interviews, the second site to contact you ideally will offer flexibility in arranging an alternate date or scheduling a Skype interview. But what if they don't? You have several options. One is to simply wait a few days and ask again. An administrative coordinator instructed to deliver a firm message regarding the absence of an alternate date may become more flexible once the site recognizes how many of their applicants will be unable to come on the preferred interview date. Another option is to write to the training director to explain your dilemma. In doing so, you may wish to emphasize your unwavering interest in the site and your integrity in maintaining your professional commitments. Here are some suggested talking points:

- You are very interested and have been working really hard to find a way to make it work.
- It is unfortunate, but flight schedules and so on seem to be making it impossible to be there for the scheduled day.
- You are disappointed because you remain really interested but you do not want to shirk your commitments you had already made to other places.
- You would love if there was any chance to do a Skype or phone interview.
- Please advise whether there is any way to remain under consideration.

Dilemma 4. You are unable to make it to your interview on the scheduled date because of weather delays or another unexpected event.

Solution. Unless all your interviews are local and perhaps scheduled exclusively within a tropical environment, you will likely find that travel delays or severe weather will lead to a change in plans. It's recommended that you communicate clearly, frequently, and compassionately if/when this occurs. Although this is your first experience with internship interviews, remember that sites have been through this many years and likely have contingency plans or flexibility for unexpected events. There is no need to panic, send repeated e-mails, or leave dozens of messages—nor is it wise to simply disappear without making your whereabouts known. When you do make contact, try to remain as flexible, open-minded, and have a good sense of humor when possible. Your travel delay may be offering an interview site an in vivo test of your grace under pressure, and the way you manage a change in plans may become valuable information to those who are interviewing you.

Interview Formats

Expect a range of interview formats, which are usually influenced by how a site defines and prefers to assess the fit between candidates and the site.

Open house "interviews." Some sites welcome all applicants to visit the internship site as part of an open house. These open houses generally are optional and informal. For many sites, attendance at the open house is not mandatory and may not increase your chances of being selected. Often the open house is not a true interview; it is simply an opportunity for you to visit the site to obtain information about a program that could not be conveyed in a brochure or by telephone. Some may not even ask you to wear name tags, to emphasize that they are not evaluating you during the open house at all. You may find it difficult to schedule one-on-one interviews with potential supervisors during the open house meeting. Sites that offer open houses may follow up with formal in-person or telephone interviews.

Telephone interviews. Some sites conduct telephone interviews exclusively, whereas others may offer a telephone interview to applicants who are unable to schedule an in-person interview for whatever reason. Many applicants have successfully matched at sites at which they have been able to participate in only a telephone rather than an in-person interview. This is a reasonable option for those applicants unable to travel to a site, although obviously it is not possible to view the facility without the in-person visit.

Telephone interviews usually last from 30 minutes to 1 hour. They are usually conducted by the training director and one or more staff psychologists involved in training. The current interns tend not to be involved in telephone interviews, although they may be, depending on the site. Many telephone interviews are structured. That is, all candidates are asked the same questions in the same order and manner. You will not have the opportunity to gauge your responses on the basis of interviewer nonverbal feedback, but telephone interviews hold many advantages. You can wear whatever you want. You can take copious notes and use the program brochure or website without worrying about making sufficient eye contact and remaining visibly engaged. There is quite a bit of scheduling flexibility, and there are no travel costs.

Site visits/in-person interviews. A large majority of interviews occur in person at the internship site. The structure of the interviews can vary considerably and will range from standardized to free-flowing conversation. Group interviews, including multiple applicants and faculty members, are possible, as are one-on-one interviews that last 30 to 60 minutes, or some combination of the two. Some of your interviews will be very structured; you may be asked a series of standardized questions to assess the breadth and depth of your clinical experience. Other interviews may be extremely informal; in fact, interviews may consist of friendly conversation with a supervisor about topics unrelated to psychology. Still other interviews may focus entirely on questions that you have about the site, requiring you to maintain the conversation and fill the interview time with many good questions. Over the years, the most common piece of feedback we have heard from applicants is that they were surprised at how much they were expected to ask the questions on interviews, rather than be asked. Your meetings may take place in a faculty member's office, while you are touring the facility, or during a lunch. You may even have the chance to explore the facility on your own. Some sites will have a full day of interviews scheduled for you, with meetings from breakfast through the end of the day. Other sites may schedule only two or three appointments with faculty or interns. Whatever the format, remember that you are being evaluated every moment you are at the site. Therefore, pay attention to how you treat support staff and your colleagues who are also interviewing. Many sites provide information about how they interview in their listing within the *APPIC Directory Online.*

Interview Checklist: Before You Go

- It is a good idea to bring along a copy of the site materials on your interview so that you may review them before beginning the interview day. Interviewers usually prefer to spend the meeting time discussing information that you could not have obtained from their site brochure. A quick review of the site materials will also help remind you of the experiences that made you most interested in the site when you applied.
- A review of your application also is helpful before beginning the interview day. You will undoubtedly be asked to discuss your perceptions regarding the fit between your interests and the training opportunities at the site. It is best to review the points you stated in your cover letter to prepare for this question.
- In many cases, you will know more about the training site than each interviewer knows about you. Bring along a few copies of your curriculum vitae (CV)—you may be asked for them. Do not assume that those interviewing you will remember your application materials well, will have read them recently, or even at all! Do not be offended by this. Simply introduce yourself anew and with the same enthusiasm you had when you submitted your application materials.
- Sites that emphasize research as well as clinical training might offer an opportunity to meet with a potential research supervisor. Much as you did when applying for graduate programs, you may want to review potential supervisors' research abstracts to help you develop informed questions regarding their work. Keep in mind that for most clinical internships, including many research-oriented internship sites, a thorough review of supervisors' research is not necessary.
- Many applicants have questions regarding appropriate attire for the internship interview. The answer is simple: Dress professionally—whatever that means for you. As a benchmark, it may be helpful to know that most male applicants wear a jacket and tie on the interview day; many wear a suit. Female applicants should consider wearing a dress or suit, dress shoes (with hosiery), and small jewelry. Dress as you would if you were on a job interview (you are!). However, it is important that you be comfortable and genuine. Resist the urge to wear an item of clothing or jewelry that will help you to "stand out" from among the other applicants; instead, attempt to differentiate yourself on the basis of your qualifications, social skills, enthusiasm, and unique fit with the site.
- Perhaps most important, review the site materials (or website) thoroughly before you attend the interview. Asking questions regarding issues that are thoroughly described on the site website sends a clear message that you are unprepared for the interview or that you are not very interested in the site. Do your homework!

THE "BIG 3"   Worries about internship interview etiquette often are unnecessary. Should you accept a cup of coffee if it is offered? Should your CV be printed on white or ivory paper? What's most important is thorough preparation and impressive delivery, and the ability to demonstrate good interpersonal skills. If you have been selected for an interview, you already likely possess the minimal qualifications needed to gain admission to the internship site. The interview process is a sorting process to help sites and applicants determine the extent to which there is a fit. You may often find that the focus is less on your credentials and more on your general demeanor and interests. If you effectively communicate that you are high in social skills, enthusiasm, and fit (i.e., the "Big 3"), then you have succeeded on the interview.

Social Skills

This seems obvious, and it is. Simply be appropriate, professional, and considerate. Use your clinical skills. Some interviews will be conversations about the location of the internship, about your experiences as a graduate student or about people you both know professionally. Have fun and use genuine humor! And if you get tired, remember, just be a LOSER:

> **L** – **L**ean forward
> **O** – **O**pen posture—do not cross your arms over yourself
> **S** – **S**it straight and squarely
> **E** – Maintain **e**ye contact
> **R** – **R**elax

You may be someone with fantastic social skills in everyday life who occasionally misplaces those skills when feeling anxious. This is quite common, and otherwise congenial people become overly distracted by self-monitoring ("Did my last response sound stupid?"), intrusive thoughts ("Did I print out my boarding pass for tonight's flight?"), and simple exhaustion ("If I have to talk about my dissertation to one more person, I will have to check into this site as a patient!"). For these reasons, it is absolutely, definitely, extremely, super important that you role play, role play, role play before you begin the interview circuit. In fact, the role play is so important, it deserves additional discussion here.

Imagine working for years to get your doctoral degree, paying hundreds of dollars to apply for internship, successfully obtaining interviews at a variety of your top sites, flying across the country to a range of places, and then learning on Match Day that you have gone unplaced. This is scary, yet it is exactly what happens to a remarkably large number of applicants who made one simple mistake: They forgot to do a 15-minute mock interview. This brief role play can really make a huge difference, and there are several reasons why.

First, a role play (with a faculty mentor if possible) is a terrific exposure exercise! Professionals in many fields use psychological science and behavioral exposure theories to prepare for big events. It would be ironic if you didn't for a psychology position, right?

Second, cognitive science suggests that rehearsal for interviews will yield different results if we practice out loud rather than simply "in our heads." Rehearsal of your talking points out loud will literally change the way you will respond to interview questions when they matter the most. Ideally, you will engage in a mock interview role play with a trusted colleague. But even if it involves talking aloud to a pet or throw pillow, it still will be beneficial.

Last, a role play often yields valuable feedback and self-observation that enables you to correct potentially off-putting habits or incoherent responses. This brief

15-minute exercise can be one of the most important tasks you engage in during this application process.

A mock interview or role play can be easy! Simply ask someone to ask you 5 to 10 minutes of standard questions you know the answers to (e.g., your dissertation topic, your career plans, your internship goals), and try and respond to each one naturally. Then, ask that same person to make up a few responses to a half-dozen questions you ask about the (mock) interview site. Within about 15 minutes, you will have collected valuable information about your own social skills within an interview context and helped prepare for the interviews to come in a way that will pay many dividends over the following 2 months.

Enthusiasm

You will likely be tired—OK, exhausted—from travel or travel delays. You may have several interviews in just a week and may find it difficult to remember the most pertinent facts about each site. You may have decided that a different site is your first choice and find it hard to appear interested in anyplace else. This is when it is most important to remember to convey enthusiasm to your hosts.

Internship sites would like to select someone who will be happy to be at their site, who will smile and have a positive attitude every day at work, and who seems energetic about the rotations and other opportunities. During the interview, let them know that you are the exact type of person they are seeking.

Following are some examples of bad and better responses to common interview questions that will help you convey enthusiasm.

Bad No. 1

Interviewer: Welcome to Internship X. Did you have any trouble getting here?

You: Well, my plane was canceled last night because of the storm, and I actually just flew out here at 6:00 this morning. I'm tired and angry at the airline. I always have problems with X airline. What about you? Do you hate X airline? At any rate, I hope this interview is worth it.

Better No. 1

Interviewer: Welcome to Internship X. Did you have any trouble getting here?

You: I was a little concerned with that storm yesterday, but I am excited to be here on time.

Bad No. 2

Interviewer: We do a lot of work with adults who have chronic schizophrenia. Do you have any experience with this population?

You: Actually, I don't. Will that be negotiable?

Better No. 2

Interviewer: We do a lot of work with adults who have chronic schizophrenia. Do you have any experience with this population?

You: No, I haven't had a chance to do that yet, but I think that would be a great experience for me because I realize it is important to have exposure to various treatment methodologies for severely mentally ill patients.

Bad No. 3

Interviewer: This rotation will involve a lot of assessment with children, and I see that you already have a lot of that experience. Is that something you are OK with?

You: Yeah, I guess. I figured I'd have to do more of that on internship, and that's fine if I have to do it.

Better No. 3

Interviewer: This rotation will involve a lot of assessment with children, and I see that you already have a lot of that experience. Is that something you are OK with?

You: I enjoy assessment, and I think that it would be good for me to develop that as a specialty. That sounds like it would be a great opportunity for me at this point in my training.

Fit

You must emphasize that you are a unique fit to the internship site. It is a big mistake to believe that the fit is clear or obvious simply because you have similar training experiences or because others in your graduate program previously were placed at that site. Remember that the faculty members may interview five or 10 times as many applicants as they have slots, and it is likely that they may have spent less time with your application than you have spent looking over their site materials. You need to show them the fit—explicitly. Some examples of bad and better responses include the following:

Bad No. 1

Interviewer: What can I tell you about the rotation I supervise here at the Veterans Affairs (VA)?

You: Well, you tell me. What would an intern's experiences be on your rotation?

Better No. 1

Interviewer: What can I tell you about the rotation I supervise here at the VA?

You: Actually, a primary goal for me is to get experience working in a VA. I think I may want to work in this kind of position one day. So, I am particularly interested in this rotation. What would a typical intern's experience be like here?

Bad No. 2

Interviewer: Hi. You must have been asked a lot of questions already, so why don't I let you ask me something? What do you want to know?

You: OK, um, I dunno, um, do you like being here in Montana?

Better No. 2

Interviewer: Hi. You must have been asked a lot of questions already, so why don't I let you ask me something? What do you want to know?

You: OK. Well, because I am really interested in getting experience with A, B, and C on internship, I was especially excited to hear about Rotations A, B, and C. They seem to be a perfect fit with my interests and skills. I have never lived in Montana, however. What is that like?

Bad No. 3

Interviewer: You come from a behavioral program, but this rotation involves a lot of experience with the Rorschach. Do you think you will fit here?

You: I am a quick learner. I've heard the Rorschach is fairly easy, and I think I will fit just fine here.

Better No. 3

Interviewer: You come from a behavioral program, but this rotation involves a lot of experience with the Rorschach. Do you think you will fit here?

You: Interesting you should mention that. One of my goals for internship was to approach assessment from a broader perspective, so the opportunity to get Rorschach experience would be a great fit for me.

A list of sample questions that you may be asked during interviews is included in Exhibit 5.1. It may be helpful for you to write out some talking points to these questions to help crystallize your thoughts. Revisit your answers after a week or two, and determine whether they are an accurate and good reflection of you, your experiences, and your interests. Practice these responses aloud; you will be surprised to find that it is initially difficult to articulate your responses smoothly and confidently.

ASK, ASK, AND ASK AGAIN

You will be asked many questions on the interview day, and your responses will help sites get to know you better and assess their ability to provide you with meaningful and helpful training. You will also have a chance to ask questions. In fact, you will likely have more interviews during which you are the inquisitor rather than the respondent, so it is essential that you be prepared with many questions about the site. Lists of sample questions for faculty and interns are included here (see Exhibits 5.2 and 5.3, respectively), but remember that these lists may be used by many applicants—so do not ask these questions verbatim. Use this list to help generate some unique questions of your own.

The manner in which you ask these questions should capture the same themes as noted earlier and help continue to communicate that you are socially skilled, enthusiastic, and a good fit. Examples of bad and better questions include the following.

Bad No. 1

You: So, you're the supervisor for the attention-deficit/hyperactivity disorder (ADHD) rotation. Can you tell me about it?

Exhibit 5.1. *Questions You May Be Asked*

1. Tell me about yourself.
   - Consider your response in separate parts.
   - Start with professional interests and goals, but consider saying, "I'd also be happy to talk about some of my personal interests." (This shows that you are multidimensional, that is, you do have a life outside of psychology.)
2. Why did you apply to our program?
   - Outline goals and training match
   - Rotations
   - Your training experiences
   - Their setting
   - Research, if applicable
   - Any extras or unique opportunities
3. What do you want to get out of our internship (training goals)?
   - Investment in training (e.g., it fits well, you have studied their brochure, and it feels right)
   - Multidisciplinary setting—excellent training ground
   - You can make contributions (describe), plus learn, gain more experience, obtain guidance, and develop expertise
   - Mentorship and good professional relationships with faculty
4. What things do you want to work on during internship?
5. What research would you want to pursue here?
6. What is the status of your dissertation?
7. Why did you choose clinical/counseling psychology?
8. What are the strengths of your graduate program?
9. What are the limitations of your graduate program?
10. Why should we select you as an intern? Match with program?
11. Tell me about your
    - Clinical experience
    - Assessment experience
    - Research experience
    - Most difficult client situation and how you handled it
12. What is your primary theoretical orientation? Why?
13. What would you be doing if you were not in psychology?
14. What are your personal strengths and weaknesses?
15. What are your clinical strengths and weaknesses?
16. What are your professional (collegial) strengths and weaknesses?
17. What population have you found it most difficult to work with?
18. Has any client or patient ever challenged your fundamental beliefs about life? What was that experience like? How did you manage it?
19. What are you looking for in supervision?
20. Who was your favorite supervisor? Why?
21. Who was your least favorite supervisor? Why?
22. Tell me about a negative supervisory experience.
23. Tell me about a rewarding supervisory experience.
24. How do you work with and understand people with different ethnic or cultural backgrounds?
25. Do you have a master's degree? In what?
26. What nonpsychology work experience has helped to shape your professional identity?
27. Why did you select the dissertation topic that you did?
28. Tell me about an ethical problem that you faced and how you handled it.
29. What are your future goals in psychology?
30. Where do you think the profession is heading?
31. What do you think about prescription privileges (or any other hot national psychology topic)?
32. What is your favorite or most influential psychology book?
33. What is your favorite nonpsychology book?
34. What else would you like me to know about you that is not on your curriculum vitae?
35. What do you do in your spare time?
36. Tell me about your most rewarding case.
37. Tell me about your toughest case.

Exhibit 5.2. *Questions to Ask Internship Faculty*

1. What is a typical day like for an intern here?
2. What are you looking for in an intern?
3. What has the impact of managed care been on the program (if applicable)? How has it affected the rotation(s)? Affected the length of stay? Affected the role of the intern?
4. Do you anticipate changes in your program in the next year (rotations, staff)?
5. What is the relationship between psychology and psychiatry departments here? Other disciplines?
6. What do you think the strengths of this internship are?
7. What do interns usually do after internship?
8. Are there opportunities for postdocs here? (Conveys that you are excited about internship and your career; will be applying for postdocs, jobs, and so forth.)
   - What kind of professional guidance is offered?
   - Are they supportive through the postdoc and job-seeking process?
   - Does the internship play an active role in trying to place its graduates?
9. Ask if not explained in materials
   - Seminars and educational opportunities or didactics and typical topics?
   - Intern evaluation process? Quality? Frequency? By whom?
   - Do they strive for breadth or specialty training?
10. Treatment opportunities
    - Individual/group/families/couples/age ranges?
    - Specific populations?
    - Typical referral questions on a specific rotation?
    - Proportion of inpatient and outpatient?
    - Continuity of care? Can you follow the patient from an inpatient stay on an outpatient basis?
    - Inpatient severity of pathology? Length of stay? Role of intern on the unit?
    - How are rotations assigned?
    - How are patients assigned to treatments? Flexibility in assignments?
11. Supervision
    - How are supervisors assigned?
    - Individual/group?
    - Hours per week or case?
    - Live? Video? Audio?
    - How many supervisors does each intern have?
    - Theoretical orientation of supervisors? Which is most strongly represented?
12. Assessment
    - Center's assessment philosophy?
    - Availability?
    - Typical frequency?
    - Emphasis?
    - Neuropsychology?
    - Opportunities outside of rotations?
    - Projectives?
    - Proportion of assessment to therapy?
13. Research
    - How strong of an emphasis do you place on research?
    - What are the opportunities for research?
    - How are research topics selected?
    - What activities might you have the opportunity to become involved with?
    - "I understand you are conducting research in X. Would an incoming intern have the opportunity to work with you in that area?"
14. Resources
    - Computer support?
    - Office?
    - Treatment rooms?
    - Referral agencies?
15. Is there ever a need to travel to other satellite clinics?
16. Are interns ever on call after hours?
17. How are emergencies managed? What is the typical frequency of emergencies?

Exhibit 5.3. *Questions to Ask the Current Interns*

1. Example of a workday/week: Typical activities? Hours per day/week? Meetings? Didactics?
   - Amount of work you take home?
   - What types of assessments?
   - How much time on assessment?
   - How many assessments per week? Write them at work or at home?
2. How is time divided among assessment, treatment, consultation, and psychotherapy?
3. Role of interns at site? With faculty?
4. Relationship between interns and faculty?
   - Do you feel that you are highly regarded by the faculty?
   - Supervision satisfaction?
   - Availability? On site if you encounter a problem?
5. Strengths of the program? Best thing?
6. Limitations/disappointments with the program? Worst thing?
7. Physical resources: Computer? Office space? Treatment rooms? Phone? Beeper?
8. On-call hours?
9. Paperwork?
10. Health care
    - Quality?
    - Satisfactory?
11. Time to work on dissertation?
12. Rotations
    - What rotations are you doing?
    - Most rewarding?
    - Least rewarding?
    - Support among the interns?
    - Number of interns on rotations at a time (one or more than one)?
    - Hours?
    - Supervision?
13. Cost of living?
14. Availability of affordable housing?
15. Do you like the city?
16. Do you socialize with faculty? With other interns?
17. Time for fun?
18. What has your experience at the site been like?
19. What has helped and impeded your adjustment to the site?
20. Where are you from? What program? What type of program?
21. What influenced your decision to select this internship?
22. For you, a year ago, what didn't you ask that would be important to know?

Better No. 1

You: I have been looking forward to meeting you because I am especially excited about the ADHD rotation. Can you tell me what opportunities interns have on this rotation?

Bad No. 2

You: Do people actually enjoy living in Idaho? Is there anything to do for fun around here?

Better No. 2

You: Living in Idaho would be a new experience for me. Can you tell me what you have enjoyed about this location?

Bad No. 3

You: Do most people get jobs in private practice when they leave this internship?

Better No. 3

You: I am really looking forward to beginning my private practice after internship, and I hear that this site offers good training experiences to help with that. Has that been the experience of most prior interns?

Bad No. 4

You: I hear that there is not much data out there supporting the incremental validity of measures like the Rorschach beyond what one could learn from a good diagnostic interview. How come y'all still administer that measure?

Better No. 4

You: I come from a program that does not emphasize training in projective assessments, but I notice that is a large component of the rotation that you supervise. What is your position on the recent debates regarding evidence-based assessment and treatment?

PURPOSE AND
GOALS OF THE
INTERVIEW

In the end, the interview provides you with an opportunity to elaborate on your strengths and weaknesses, or in other words, the opportunities that exist for you to be further trained. The interview allows you to further articulate and define your training goals and how the site can help you reach them. The site is assessing how trainable you are for their site. If they are unable to find an area in which they can teach you, then they will consider you a poor fit for their site. Although it may not always seem like it, remember that you are also interviewing the site. After all, you will be making a large investment of time and even money to intern at a particular site. You need to find a site where you will feel comfortable, be able to develop and grow your skills, and fit in. This is an opportunity for you to identify common clinical and research interests and truly become excited about teaming up together for a year. And, sometimes most important, a site wants to learn through the interview that you are likeable, easy to work with, open to feedback, and normal!

THANK-YOU
NOTES

Opinions vary about whether you should send a thank-you note or other correspondence to follow-up after an interview. Thank-you notes certainly are not required or necessary, and the presence or absence of a note or particular type of note (e.g., e-mail, typed letter, handwritten notecard, hologram delivered by carrier pigeon) will rarely influence the decision of the admissions committee. We suggest that you send a follow-up if it is consistent with your interpersonal style and feels like something you'd like to do. Thank-you notes can be a courteous, appropriate way to express gratitude to your hosts, and therefore the practice is quite common among intern applicants.

In addition to an expression of gratitude, thank-you notes offer a final opportunity to express your interest in the site and explicitly state your perception of the fit between the site and your interests or training goals. Let the note be an extension of your own style and the level of professionalism that you have communicated throughout the application process. Several sample thank-you notes have been included at the end of this chapter as examples, should you wish to send one.

Applicants often face a dilemma when deciding whether to send separate thank-you notes to each person with whom they interviewed at one site or to send a note only to the training director. Again, there is no right or wrong answer. E-mail notes can be easily forwarded to many, but individually typed letters to more than a dozen faculty members at a site may be a bit excessive.

A few suggestions when writing thank-you notes include the following:

- Thank-you notes may demonstrate initiative and genuine interest, and they may help to make you memorable. Keep them simple, and make them personal if you are able.
- Follow-up can be another opportunity to highlight something positive about your CV, experience, training, or interview. Send your note within a day or so after your interview so you will be fresh on the mind of the individual who receives your note.

January 24, 2018

Dear Dr. X,

I enjoyed meeting with you on January 16, and I am very impressed with your program. Speaking with you, Dr. Y, Dr. Z, and the current interns was helpful to me in forming a more complete understanding of the XXX Consortium.

Overall, I believe that the rotations and experiences offered at XXX match my goals for internship training. Additionally, the pediatric research opportunities are another attractive aspect of your training program.

In addition to the variety of training opportunities, I was greatly impressed by the friendliness and warmth of the people at XXX. I believe that I would be happy and honored to work with everyone with whom I met during my visit.

I am very enthusiastic about my visit to XXX. As per our conversation on January 23, I believe that XXX provides an optimal fit with my previous experiences and future interests for internship training.

Sincerely,

Your Name

Sample Thank-You Note 2

February 1, 2018

Dear Dr. X,

I wanted to thank you for taking the time to meet with me to discuss my internship application and your program. After hearing so many positive things about the internship from friends and colleagues, it was nice to leave the interview day with the same positive feelings myself!

I am very impressed with and excited about the training opportunities your internship has to offer. I feel that your internship's strong adherence to the scientist–practitioner model, with attention devoted to both clinical and research training, is unique among the internship programs I have explored. XXX seems like an ideal place for me to gain breadth in my clinical training, as well as have the opportunity to apply my research skills to areas in pediatric psychology other than studying pediatric pain. Some of the research projects we discussed (e.g., familial transmission in pediatric obesity) were incredibly interesting and exciting to me!

Again, thank you for your time, and I hope that you will consider me for your fine internship.

Sincerely,

Your Name

Sample Thank-You Note 3

January 20, 2018

Dear Dr. X,

Thank you for taking the time to meet with me to discuss my internship application and your program. I enjoyed the tour of the hospital and also appreciated hearing about your work; the training opportunities available in the sleep disorders clinic sounded particularly interesting! I am very impressed with your internship program and think that XXX would be an ideal place for me to continue my clinical and research training.

Again, thank you for your time, and I hope that you will continue to consider me for your internship.

Sincerely,

Your Name

January 30, 2018

Dear Dr. X and Dr. Y,

I appreciated the opportunity to interview with you over the telephone. I was especially struck by the important questions you asked about clinical competency in diversity issues that were embedded in the vignettes posed. Since the telephone interview, I have continued to think about your site, the vignettes, and your brochure. The more I think about the training opportunities at your site, the more excited I become with the thought of being matched to XXX.

I look forward to having the opportunity to meet you in person—I hope by being matched to your site.

Thank you for the invitation to call or write with further questions regarding your internship site. As I learn more about your training philosophy and internship site, I become more and more convinced that XXX would be an ideal match for me.

Sincerely,

Your Name

6 THE MATCH

Once your internship interviews have been completed, the next step is to begin thinking about how to navigate the Association of Psychology Postdoctoral and Internship Centers (APPIC) Match. The Match was first implemented in 1999 by APPIC to deal with an internship selection process that, frankly, had become a nightmare for applicants. Before then, applicants had to endure pressure tactics, game playing, and indirect or inappropriate communication by internship sites. Although the Match has not made internship selection stress free, it has made a huge difference in the lives of applicants.

The Match may seem somewhat daunting at first; however, you will find it to be an easy, straightforward, and user-friendly process. This chapter provides an overview of that process, along with tips about how to make the Match work best for you.

AN OVERVIEW OF THE APPIC MATCH

The APPIC Match is a fair and efficient process for placing psychology graduate students into internship positions based solely on the stated preferences of applicants and programs. It is administered by National Matching Services, Inc. (NMS), a Toronto-based company that specializes in professional matching services and is the leading provider of matching programs for a variety of professions and industries. It uses an algorithm that was developed by Alvin Roth and Elliott Peranson (president of NMS) that was instrumental in Roth winning the Nobel Prize in Economics in 2012. This algorithm ensures that every participant receives the best matches possible from the available options.

The Match is currently conducted in two "phases"—essentially two separate matches, conducted one right after the other. Phase I of the Match typically occurs from October through February and includes all applicants who wish to participate

http://dx.doi.org/10.1037/0000102-006

http://dx.doi.org/10.1037/0000102-006
Internships in Psychology: The APAGS Workbook for Writing Successful Applications and Finding the Right Fit, Fourth Edition, by C. Williams-Nickelson, M. J. Prinstein, and W. G. Keilin

and all positions that are registered and available. Phase I is when the vast majority of applicants get placed. Phase II begins immediately upon the conclusion of Phase I and includes applicants who were unmatched in Phase I and positions that were unfilled in Phase I. Phase II can be thought of as an accelerated, second-chance opportunity for students who were unable to secure an internship position during Phase I.

So, each phase is actually its own separate placement/matching process, each with the following steps: (a) application submission, (b) interviews, (c) constructing and submitting a rank order list (ROL), and (d) distribution of the Match results.

Match Eligibility

As noted in Chapter 1, significant changes were made by APPIC to the Match eligibility policy, effective for the 2018–2019 training year. Students who are enrolled in such nonaccredited doctoral programs should check the Match section of the APPIC website for the most up-to-date eligibility policies in case things have changed since this workbook was published. We also encourage them to consult with their doctoral faculty for assistance in identifying options for obtaining an internship.

Timeline

Your participation in the APPIC Match occurs at several distinct times during the internship selection process:

Date	*Activity*
March 15 (or earlier)	Subscribe to the Match-News e-mail list.
August through December 1	Register for the APPIC Match.
Late January to early February	Construct and submit your ROL for Phase I of the Match.
Late February	Receive your Match results.
Late February through late March	Phase II of the Match is conducted.

Each of these activities is described in detail in this chapter.

Subscribing to Match-News

APPIC sponsors a free e-mail list service, called Match-News, that provides valuable information about the Match (along with tips and suggestions about the application process) directly from the APPIC Match coordinator. American Psychological Association of Graduate Students (APAGS) leaders and staff subscribe to this list to monitor announcements and changes in the process. It is strongly recommended that all applicants subscribe to this list as early as possible in the process (ideally by March 15 of the year in which you intend to apply, though some applicants subscribe 1 or 2 years earlier to familiarize themselves with the process). Match-News is a low-volume list, so you usually will receive no more than five e-mail messages per month.

To subscribe to Match-News, first send a blank e-mail to subscribe-match-news@ lyris.appic.org. Shortly after sending this e-mail, you should receive a return e-mail requesting that you confirm your subscription. Once you have completed that confirmation process, you should receive a "welcome" message from the list, which indicates that you have successfully subscribed and will receive future messages. Once subscribed, you can review previous messages that were posted to the list by following the instructions in the "E-mail Lists" section of the APPIC website (http://www.appic.org). More information about APPIC's e-mail lists, including a discussion list for applicants called "Intern-Network," may be found here as well.

MATCH REGISTRATION

Match registration typically opens in late July or early August. To register for the Match, simply go to the Match website (http://www.natmatch.com/psychint) and complete the online registration process. To have your registration properly processed, it is very important that you identify your school, doctoral program, degree earned, and director of clinical training (DCT) accurately. The Match registration fee covers your participation in both phases of the Match; in other words, if you need to participate in Phase II, you will not need to register again, and you will not be charged another registration fee. Please note that registering for the Match is an entirely separate process from registering for the APPIC Application for Psychology Internships (AAPI) Online service.

During the Match registration process, you will be assigned a five-digit applicant code number that uniquely identifies you for the purposes of the Match. You will also be assigned a confidential password that will allow you to access the important functions of the Match website, such as submitting your ROL and obtaining your Match result. Keep this password in a secure place. Once you have registered for the Match, be sure to enter your applicant code number into the designated area of your application within the AAPI Online service.

Although APPIC recommends that applicants register for the Match no later than December 1, it is a good idea to register by mid- to late October so that you will receive your applicant code number in time to include it on your AAPI. Remember, though, that the registration fee is nonrefundable and not transferable to another selection year. Thus, if you are unsure about whether you will be participating in the APPIC Match this year (e.g., if you are unsure if you will meet your department's requirements in time, or if you aren't certain that you will be pursuing an internship during this cycle), you might want to wait until later in the process to register, once those uncertainties have been resolved. If you do not register for the Match prior to submitting your internship applications, don't worry—simply enter your applicant code number into the AAPI Online service once you have registered. If you register after December 31, you must submit written approval from your DCT.

Once you have completed your registration, you will not need to think much more about the Match until you have finished the interviewing process.

PHASE I OF THE MATCH

Constructing Your Rank Order List

After the whirlwind of interviewing in December and January comes to a close and you have a chance to evaluate each of your potential internship programs, you will need to determine your order of preference for these programs. Ultimately, you will need to develop a ROL for the Match, which is a list of internship programs to which you have applied in the order in which you prefer them.

One important consideration that we cannot overemphasize is the following: The order in which you rank internship programs should reflect only your true preferences, without regard for how you think these programs have ranked you, whether the programs will be ranking you, or what sort of pressure you might have experienced from others to rank programs. Thus, the program that you are most excited about should be ranked first on your ROL, your next most preferred program should be ranked second, and so forth.

Why is it so important for you to rank programs in the order in which you truly prefer them? The Match algorithm has been specifically designed to allow you to think only about your own needs and preferences, providing an opportunity for you to make ranking decisions in as pressure-free an environment as possible. The computer has been programmed to respect your rankings, and you will be matched to the highest-ranked program on your list that ranks you and does not fill its positions with more-preferred applicants. If you deviate from using your true preferences—for example, by trying to guess how a site has ranked you and adjusting your rankings on the basis of this assumption—you will likely end up hurting yourself because you could end up being matched to a less-preferred program. You will receive the best outcome only if you rank programs in the order in which you want to attend them.

Many applicants worry about not being matched, and such concerns can be a significant source of temptation to submit an ROL that doesn't reflect one's true preferences. However, it's important to know that the order of your rankings will affect only where you are matched, not whether you will be matched. In other words, if the ROL that you submit results in your not being matched, then you can know that the same unfortunate outcome would have occurred if you had submitted an ROL with those same programs ordered differently. Changing the order of your rankings will not increase or decrease your chances of being matched (although, of course, it could affect where you get matched). Thus, submitting an ROL that reflects something other than your true preferences is a very poor strategy.

It is unfortunate that APPIC occasionally hears of rumors that contradict the advice provided above. If you hear such rumors, or if you have questions about any aspect of the ranking process, feel free to contact the APPIC Match coordinator directly for assistance. Some additional points to remember about constructing your ROL are outlined below.

- You may rank as many programs as you wish.
- Your rankings remain confidential. Internship programs will never be told where you have ranked them, either before or after the Match.
- In general, you should rank all the programs at which you are being considered. However, you should omit any program from your list that you consider unacceptable. In other words, if you do not want to be matched to a particular program under any circumstances, simply omit that program from your ROL. You cannot be matched to any program that is not listed on your ROL.
- You should remember that the results of the Match are binding, which means that you are required to attend the internship program to which you are matched. And, although most applicants are matched to one of their highly ranked programs, it is possible for you to be matched to any program that is included on your ROL. So, again, do not include a program on your ROL if you do not want to be matched to that program.

- Each program in the Match has a six-digit "program code number" that must be used when constructing your rankings. A list of participating programs and their program code numbers is available on the NMS website after November 1 of each year.
- Some internship sites may have more than one program code number, usually to represent different rotations or training experiences. For example, a site with a neuropsychology rotation and a geropsychology rotation may use a different program code number for each, allowing you to rank the programs separately on your ROL. Sites should clarify for you (in their written materials or during the interview process) how their program code numbers are affiliated with which programs, rotations, or training experiences.

To better illustrate the ranking process, let's say that you have applied to several internship programs, and your true preferences for these programs dictate that you rank them in the following order:

Your True Preferences

999901—Really Fine Community Mental Health Center (CMHC)
888801—Better Health Hospital: Neuropsychology Program
777701—Truly Wonderful Medical Center
888802—Better Health Hospital: Geropsychology Program
666601—Sunshine Hospital

In this illustration, you have decided to rank two separate programs at the Better Health Hospital using each program's unique program code number. Because you prefer the neuropsychology program over the geropsychology program, these rankings reflect this preference.

Let's throw some twists into this scenario with a couple of examples.

Example 1. Let's say that Sunshine Hospital calls you and tells you that you are a truly wonderful applicant and offers you free housing and a boat to use during your internship year. In fact, they violate Match policies and tell you that they are ranking you as their number one choice.

Question: Given this situation, should you move Sunshine Hospital higher on your ROL so you don't "miss out" on them?

Answer: Absolutely not. Because your true preference is for Sunshine Hospital to be ranked fifth, the best and only approach is to leave them ranked fifth. If Sunshine Hospital does rank you as their number one choice, you will definitely be matched to them only if the computer is unable to match you to the four higher ranked programs on your list. In other words, you haven't reduced your chances of getting matched to Sunshine Hospital by ranking your more-preferred programs higher on your list.

Example 2. Let's say that the Really Fine CMHC doesn't seem that interested in you. In fact, even though you got a highly favorable impression of the program during your interview, you suspect that you did a horrible job in responding to their interview questions. Despite this interview fiasco, they remain your most preferred site.

Question: Given this situation, should you move Really Fine CMHC lower on your list based on your assumption that they aren't going to rank you very highly?

Answer: Absolutely not. In this situation, you should definitely rank Really Fine CMHC as number one on your list.

If the computer is not successful in matching you to Really Fine CMHC, it will simply go to the next site on your list without having penalized you in any way. In other words, by ranking the Really Fine CMHC as number one, you have not reduced your chances of being matched to any other site on your list. Thus, you don't get penalized for ranking sites that you consider to be long shots.

Submitting Your Rank Order List

Once you have constructed your ROL, you must then log in to the NMS website (http://www.natmatch.com/psychint) to submit your rankings to the Match. To log in, use your applicant code number and the password that was previously provided to you by NMS. Entering your rankings is a simple and straightforward process, and complete instructions are available on the NMS website. Once you have finished entering your ROL, you must certify it, which designates your list as being complete and ready to use in the Match.

If you change your mind about your rankings before the ROL submission deadline, you can log in again to the NMS Match website and make the appropriate changes to your ROL. You can do this even if your list was previously certified (but be sure to recertify the list once you have made your changes). Here's a tip: Don't wait until the last day to enter your rankings! You don't want to risk being unable to access the system if you encounter internet connection problems or a busy server.

Every registered applicant must submit either an ROL or a formal withdrawal from the Match. If you do not have any programs to rank (e.g., you had the disappointing experience of not receiving any interviews or your situation has changed and you decided not to participate in the Match), then you must submit a withdrawal from the Match. This lets NMS know that you will not be participating in Phase I. Even if you withdraw from Phase I of the Match, you may still choose to participate in Phase II and/or the Post-Match Vacancy Service (PMVS).

Receiving Your Match Result

Once you have submitted your ROL for Phase I, there is nothing left to do but wait for the Match processing to take place. The wait between the ROL submission deadline and the release of the Match results is just over 2 weeks. Although the wait can be excruciating, this time period is absolutely necessary for NMS to ensure that the Match is conducted accurately. While you wait, NMS extensively checks and rechecks the Match processing to ensure that all applicants and programs receive the best possible match.

The release of the Match results for Phase I occurs in late February—generally on a Friday at 10:00 a.m. Eastern Standard Time (EST; be sure to adjust this time to your own time zone)—on a day known as "APPIC Phase I Match Day." On this day, you will learn whether you were successfully matched to an internship program and, if so, the name of the program to which you were matched. In addition, on this day, internship programs are told the names of the applicants to whom they have been matched. For applicants who aren't matched in Phase I, the second phase of the Match (described below) begins operating on this day.

Your Match results can be obtained in three ways, as described below.

- *Via e-mail:* NMS will attempt to send you an e-mail message no later than 10:00 a.m. EST on Match Day (in practice, it typically arrives an hour or two earlier). Keep in mind that e-mail is subject to delays or errors and thus is not 100% reliable (in fact, an estimated 5% of applicants do not receive this e-mail in a timely fashion). If you do not receive this e-mail, check your spam or junk mail folder. If that doesn't work, you may use one of the two additional methods to obtain your Match results.
- *Via the Internet:* Beginning at 10:00 a.m. EST on Match Day, you may use your applicant code number and password to log in to the NMS website to obtain your results.
- *Via your DCT:* Beginning at 10:00 a.m. EST on Match Day, your DCT will have access to your Match results.

On Match Day, after you have received the name of the site to which you have been matched, you will need to take care of one additional detail: Talk with your new training director! Most training directors like to talk with their new interns on this day to provide a personal welcome. Training directors and applicants are allowed to contact each other after 11:00 a.m. EST on Match Day, and training directors usually, but not always, initiate calls to their new interns after that time. You may recall that you provided a telephone number on your application where you can be reached between 11:00 a.m. and 1:00 p.m. EST on that day, and it's best to remain available at that number during that time. If you do not receive a call from your new training director during that period, it is possible that he or she is having difficulty reaching you, and you should call him or her to acknowledge the Match result.

Finally, training directors are required to send you a written appointment agreement, postmarked or e-mailed no later than 7 days after Match Day. If you have not received this agreement within 2 weeks after Match Day, contact your new training director to inquire about its status.

WHAT IF I DON'T MATCH? Without a doubt, learning that you did not get matched to an internship site is the most painful and challenging outcome of the application process. Fortunately, given the greatly reduced imbalance between the number of applicants and the number of available positions, it is a situation that fewer and fewer students are finding themselves in each year. APPIC provides two services for unmatched students to find an internship position: Phase II of the APPIC Match and the PMVS. We describe these steps later in this chapter.

It may be important at this point to take some time to reflect on the process and to identify any aspects of your application and/or interview that might be improved. Some specific suggestions:

- Consider contacting training directors at sites where you applied to request candid feedback about your application and/or interview. Although not all training directors will be willing to provide you such feedback (and some may be prevented from doing so by the policies of their Human Resources departments), many will be happy to do so. In the event that you experience some reluctance on the part of internship training directors to provide this kind of feedback, you should consider asking your DCT to contact them on your behalf.
- Review the choices that you made during your application process. Did you apply to sites that were all highly competitive? Did you apply to a limited geographic area? Did you apply to sites that may not have been good fits for your interests and/or experiences? Any of these approaches could have had a significant negative impact on your ability to be matched.
- Review your application materials and get feedback from several trusted faculty members about how they can be improved. Were your essays as compelling as they could be? Was there anything in your cover letter or essays that may have come across in a way other than you attended? Did any of your recommenders write a weak letter? Did you have sufficient practicum hours and experiences to be competitive? Although certain portions of your AAPI cannot be changed for Phase II, other aspects (e.g., cover letters, essays, references) can be modified.
- Work on improving your interviewing skills, for example, through mock interviews or a similar process.

OTHER THINGS TO KNOW

APPIC Match Policies

APPIC has developed a set of policies that guide the operation of the Match. These policies are available for viewing or downloading on both the APPIC and NMS websites and are included with the registration instructions that you received from NMS. It is imperative that you read these policies carefully early in the process, and in particular before your interviews, as you are expected to abide by them throughout the selection process. APPIC does take action against internship programs and applicants who violate the policies. Although not a substitute for actually reading the Match policies, below are some of the more important considerations for internship applicants.

First, applicants and programs are not permitted to communicate, solicit, accept, or use any ranking-related information before the release of the Match results. Furthermore, applicants and programs may never ask about how they have been ranked, even after the release of the Match results. Some examples of what applicants should never say to an internship program include the following:

- "You are my first choice."
- "You are one of my top-ranked sites."
- "I really like your site better than the other sites at which I've interviewed."
- "Where do you intend to rank me?"

Even with these restrictions, it is important to understand that the policies are not intended to restrict the expression of genuine interest or enthusiasm about a program. So, here are some examples of what is permissible:

- "I have really enjoyed my interview with you today."
- "I am very impressed with your internship program."
- "I really like this neuropsychology rotation, and I really believe that it will meet my training needs."
- "Your internship faculty seem to be very invested in the training needs of your interns."
- "After visiting your inpatient program, I don't think it is quite what I'm looking for. However, I would still very much like to be considered for your outpatient program, as that seems to be a much better fit for me."

So, the best approach is to simply follow the normal guidelines of courteous and professional communication while not making any statements about rankings or about comparing one internship program with another.

Second, each internship program that conducts onsite or telephone interviews must notify you as to whether you will be interviewed, no later than the interview notification date listed for that program in the *APPIC Directory Online.*

Third, the results of the Match are binding. Once you submit an ROL to the Match, you are obligated to attend the internship program to which you are matched. Similarly, the program to which you are matched is required to accept you as an intern for the coming year.

Fourth, after the Match is completed, training directors are required to send you a written appointment agreement outlining the conditions of the appointment, such as stipend, fringe benefits, and the beginning and ending dates of the internship year.

Couples

The APPIC Match has special procedures to assist applicants who are members of a couple when both partners are applying for psychology internships in the same year. These procedures allow a couple to coordinate their rankings in a way that can improve their chances of being placed in the same geographic area. Any two individuals who are participating in the Match may designate themselves as a "couple" for the purposes of the Match. Although couples are not required to use these procedures, virtually all couples will find it advantageous to do so. More information about this option is available at both the APPIC and NMS websites.

Resolving Problems

APPIC has two services to assist applicants who are experiencing difficulties with the selection process or their internship experience, as described below.

- *Informal Problem Consultation:* This process allows you to consult confidentially with an APPIC representative to discuss your concerns and to identify options and solutions. If desired, APPIC may become directly involved in negotiating a resolution among parties. Over the past few years, APPIC has found this process to be a highly effective way of resolving difficulties experienced by applicants.

- *Formal Complaints:* APPIC also has a formal complaint process and has established the APPIC Standards and Review Committee to review and investigate such complaints. In response to a formal complaint, the APPIC board may impose sanctions on programs or applicants who violate APPIC policies.

Staying Informed

Several resources are available that provide additional information about the Match, answer your questions, and generally keep you informed about the process.

- Extensive information is available at the APPIC and NMS websites (http://www. natmatch.com/psychint and http://www.appic.org).
- Be sure that you subscribe to the Match-News list, as described earlier in this chapter, as early as possible in the process.
- APPIC also maintains an e-mail discussion list, Intern-Network, that allows current and former intern applicants, training directors, APPIC board members, and APAGS representatives to ask questions and to discuss various aspects of the selection process. This is a popular place for internship applicants to get answers to their questions about the AAPI, interviews, the Match, or any other aspect of the process. To subscribe, simply send a blank e-mail message to subscribe-intern-network@lyris.appic.org. Because this list can generate a lot of e-mail in busy times, you may wish to set your subscription to "digest" mode, which allows you to receive a maximum of one e-mail per day that contains all the messages that were posted to the list in the preceding 24 hours. To sign up for digest mode, first subscribe as already described, and then send a blank e-mail to digest-intern-network@lyris.appic.org.
- The APPIC Match coordinator, Dr. Greg Keilin, is always happy to answer your questions or assist you with the process. He may be contacted at gkeilin@mail. utexas.edu or (512) 410-0002.
- Questions about the AAPI Online service may be directed to either the AAPI Online coordinator (for content-related issues and questions) or to the AAPI Online technical support team. Please see the "Contact" link on the APPIC website for their current contact information.

PHASE II OF THE MATCH

So, it is the Friday in late February known as "Phase I Match Day," and you have just received that dreaded e-mail message that says, "We regret to inform you that you did not match to a position." Now what?

First and foremost, if you find yourself without a match, this is not the time to be questioning yourself, your competencies, or your suitability for the profession of psychology (even though those are normal reactions to this frustrating turn of events). It is also not the time to isolate yourself or to get stuck in your disappointment, embarrassment, anger, fear, confusion, hopelessness, or any of the myriad of emotions that you may be experiencing. Instead, talk with family, friends, fellow graduate students, and trusted faculty members about the situation and your feelings. By mobilizing your support systems, along with your energies, resources, and creativity, you will be well prepared to move forward with the next step of the process.

The fact of the matter is that unmatched applicants are typically highly competent and talented individuals. How do we know this? Because internship training directors routinely tell us that some of their best interns have been students who were unmatched during Phase I but were later placed at their site (e.g., during Phase II). In addition, literally thousands of "ex-unmatched applicants" ultimately found an internship and are now happy and settled as licensed, practicing psychologists.

Phase II is an opportunity for unmatched applicants from Phase I to apply for internship positions that were unfilled in Phase I. It is, quite simply, a second application and matching process that occurs in an accelerated fashion. Phase II lasts about a month (late February to late March) from start to finish, and it includes (a) a period for students to submit applications to sites, (b) a period for interviews to be conducted, (c) the submission of new ROLs, and (d) the distribution of Phase II Match results. No additional Match or AAPI Online fees are required to participate in Phase II.

If you registered for the Match during Phase I and did not get matched to an internship position during Phase I, then you are eligible to participate in Phase II. This is true even if you withdrew or didn't submit an ROL during Phase I. However, you must have registered during Phase I to be eligible for Phase II, as new Match registrations are not permitted during Phase II.

This section provides you with an overview of how Phase II works, and complete instructions, along with a set of Frequently Asked Questions, can be found on the APPIC (http://www.appic.org) and NMS (http://www.natmatch.com/psychint) websites.

Step 1: Preparation

First, review the timeline for Phase II. You will notice that Phase II begins at 11:00 a.m. EST on Phase I Match Day and that you have 6 days (as of this writing) to decide where to apply during Phase II and to submit your applications. Although you will likely find the 6-day period to be a sufficient amount of time to get that done, it also means that you need to begin moving forward as soon as possible. Thus, you will likely want to clear your schedule for several days, giving you the time to focus on this next step of the process.

The good news about this accelerated timeline is that internship training directors will not be able to view any Phase II applications until the end of the 6-day application period. This enables you to move through these steps in a measured way, without the pressure of having to submit your application before others do.

It is vitally important at this stage to clarify for yourself the types of internships you are willing to consider in this next phase of the process. Are you willing to consider non-accredited and/or non-APPIC member internship programs? (If you consider such programs, be sure that you understand the implications of such a decision; see Chapter 1, "Getting Started," for specifics.) Are you willing to broaden your internship search to different settings, populations, training opportunities, and so on? Where might you be willing to relocate? What is the minimum level of funding you would accept? Which of these options will be supported by your doctoral program? Thinking about these issues now, and in particular, consulting with your DCT and other faculty, will help you decide where to apply in Phase II.

Be sure to carefully review the information about Phase II on the APPIC website, including the Phase II "Getting Started" guide for applicants and the Frequently Asked Questions. Those pages contain comprehensive and specific information about how to navigate Phase II as well as feedback from previous unmatched applicants about how to make the most of the process.

Step 2: Review the List of Available Positions

Once Phase II of the Match begins, a list of programs with available positions is posted on the NMS website (http://www.natmatch.com/psychint). This list consists primarily of positions that were unfilled from Phase I of the Match, along with a few additional positions that may have come open too late to be included in Phase I (e.g., because of funding delays).

The list is organized by state or province, and then by city, and contains basic information about each program along with a link to the site's *APPIC Directory Online* listing (for sites that are APPIC members). The list is not updated once it is released, and each entry looks something like this:

BLOOMING DAISIES MENTAL HEALTH CENTER

1234 MAIN STREET
DIAGNOSIS, NEW MEXICO 12345
Telephone: (222) 222-2222
E-mail: Jane.Smith@BloomingDaisiesMHC.org
Director: Jane Smith, PhD
APPIC Member: Yes (Link to *APPIC Directory Online* Listing)
Accreditation: APA—NO CPA—NO
Program: Pediatrics
Code: 999901 Openings: 1
Program: Neuropsychology
Code: 999902 Openings: 2

In addition to this list, APPIC sponsors a "late-breaking news" service during Phase II that allows internship training directors to post news or updates about their available positions. For example, a program may want to publicize special application requirements for the available position(s), revise its selection criteria, or simply provide additional information about its vacancy(ies). These late-breaking items are available on a special page of the APPIC website, which is updated frequently as new information is received from programs. APPIC recommends that you wait until the first set of news items is posted (usually the day after Phase II begins) before submitting any applications.

When deciding where to apply, it is usually best to apply to sites that are a good fit with your interests and background. Taking a shotgun approach (i.e., applying to a large number of sites without regard for how qualified you are for those positions) is generally a poor strategy, and your time is likely better spent on carefully selecting programs that are a good fit for you and writing thoughtful cover letters. Training directors often complain that they receive many applications during Phase II from students who are clearly not qualified and/or who are poor fits for their programs, and such applications are rarely successful.

Students often wonder, during Phase II, if it is acceptable to apply to programs to which they previously applied (e.g., during Phase I). Yes, absolutely. In fact, some programs may actually prefer applicants who previously applied, even if those applicants weren't initially successful in getting an interview or being matched to that program.

Step 3: Preparing Your Applications

You will use the AAPI Online service to submit your applications in Phase II, just as you did in Phase I. In fact, the application that you used in Phase I will remain available to you during Phase II. Although the core part of your application remains locked and unchangeable, you may use the same curriculum vitae (CV), essays, and letters of recommendation, or you may submit new ones. As noted below, you will need to write a new cover letter for each program to which you apply in Phase II. Your graduate transcripts remain on file and thus do not need to be resubmitted.

One thing to consider is whether you should take the time to revise your essays, take a different approach in your cover letters, update your CV, and so on. This is a decision that should be made in consultation with your faculty, although you should remember that changes must be completed within the 6-day application submission window. It is also acceptable to ask for feedback from training directors at sites to which you submitted applications during Phase I, although getting such feedback soon enough to use to apply in Phase II can be challenging. In deciding whether to make such revisions, consider how well your applications were received during Phase I; if you received relatively few or no offers of interviews, then a revision of your application materials may be in order.

In Phase II, it is important for you to tailor your cover letters to each site to which you are applying, just as you (hopefully) did in Phase I. Thus, in Phase II, your cover letters should describe how you fit with the program and how your interests, experiences, and background are congruent with what the program has to offer.

Please note that you should not submit any supplemental materials (e.g., undergraduate transcripts, testing reports) to sites even if a site's application instructions tell you to do so. Training directors understand this limitation and will not expect your application in Phase II to include supplemental materials. Later in the process, sites may contact selected applicants from their pool and ask them to provide additional information; if you receive such a request, you will need to provide that information separately from the AAPI Online service, such as via e-mail.

Step 4: Submitting Your Applications

APPIC has established an application deadline, which is currently 6 days after Phase II begins. As previously mentioned, internship training directors will not be able to see or review any submitted applications until this deadline date. Although training directors may choose to continue receiving applications after the deadline, most will choose to shut off the submission of applications at that time. Thus, you should be sure to have all your applications submitted within the 6-day window.

To submit an application, simply follow the same steps that you used to submit an application during Phase I. You will be permitted to submit applications only to those programs that are participating in Phase II, and you won't be charged any submission fees by the AAPI Online service.

Step 5: Interviewing

Once the 6-day application phase is completed, the next 2.5 weeks involve application review and interviews by programs. Waiting to hear from sites can be challenging during this time, as the amount of time it takes to review applications will vary among sites. Some sites may not acknowledge receiving applicants' materials or notify those applicants who do not receive an interview. Although this lack of individual response may seem rude or discourteous, keep in mind that sites have a tremendous amount of work to do during this relatively brief period of time.

One way to use this time is to sharpen your interviewing skills—something that may be particularly relevant if you were offered a significant number of interviews during Phase I but didn't get matched. It is important to remember that the skills that make you a strong graduate student are actually different from the skills required to be a strong interviewee. Thus, you can be a terrific clinician, researcher, teacher, and so on, but not be as skilled in communicating those strengths during an interview. Role plays with faculty members or others can be a terrific way to get feedback and potentially strengthen your interviewing performance during Phase II.

Receiving an invitation for an interview is typically a sign that the program is seriously considering you, as sites typically conduct a relatively limited number of interviews during Phase II. Because time is limited, most programs offer applicants telephone rather than in-person interviews. However, sites that are local to you may request that you visit them in person.

Step 6: Submitting Your Rank Order List

Once you have completed your interviews, you need to submit your ROL via the NMS website. This step is essentially identical to the submission process that occurred in Phase I. The advice provided earlier in this chapter about ranking programs in the order that you prefer them is just as important in Phase II. In the unfortunate event that you did not receive any interview offers in Phase II and thus have no programs to rank, you should submit a formal withdrawal from Phase II.

Step 7: Receiving Your Phase II Match Result

The Phase II Match results are distributed in the exact same way as were the Phase I results. If you learn that you matched, congratulations! As in Phase I, your new training director will likely call you to acknowledge the Match results. In addition, she or he is required to send you a written appointment agreement within a week of the conclusion of Phase II.

THE APPIC POST-MATCH VACANCY SERVICE

If you don't get matched in Phase II, there is still another option: the PMVS. This service begins operation immediately upon the conclusion of Phase II (usually in late March) and continues throughout the Summer and into the Fall (currently through October 31). In 2017, about 100 internship programs posted nearly 200 vacant positions in the PMVS. In addition to using the PMVS to post the unfilled positions from Phase II, training directors can also post new positions that may be created after the Match as a result of additional funding. Applicants do not pay a fee to use the PMVS.

The PMVS is a much less structured process than Phases I and II, as it does not currently use the AAPI Online service or the APPIC Match and thus looks much more like a typical job application process. In a nutshell, the process is as follows.

(a) Applicants regularly review the current list of available positions on the APPIC website.
(b) When an applicant wishes to apply for a position, she or he submits the appropriate application materials to the program via e-mail.
(c) The site training director reviews applications and conducts interviews.
(d) When the program has found a suitable candidate, an offer of an internship position is made to the applicant.

Information about participating in the PMVS is provided below. Be sure to consult the APPIC website for more specific instructions as well as any changes to the procedure that may have occurred after the publication of this workbook.

Locating Vacant Positions

In the PMVS, vacancies are posted on a designated page of the APPIC website, in chronological order. APPIC also provides a special e-mail service that, once you are subscribed, will notify you via e-mail whenever that page is updated. Instructions for subscribing to this service are located on the APPIC website.

Preparing and Submitting Your Application

At the time of this writing, APPIC had just recently made some substantial changes to the application submission process for the PMVS, and more changes were likely in the near future. Thus, please refer to the APPIC website for the most up-to-date instructions for this aspect of the process.

Interviews

A program that is interested in you will contact you to arrange an interview. Typically, these interviews are scheduled for a specific date or time, but it's also possible that a program may request that you interview "on the spot"—that is, while they have you on the phone. On rare occasions, a site may want you to come for an on-site interview, and it is up to you as to whether you want to devote the time and incur the expense of such travel.

Receiving an Offer

A site that wants to offer you a position will generally do so via telephone. In fact, some applicants receive an offer at the conclusion of their telephone interview! Be sure that you are clear about all terms of employment (e.g., salary, benefits, duties of the position) before accepting an offer. The training director is required by APPIC policies to send you an employment agreement, postmarked within one week of your acceptance.

Remember, once an offer has been made by a program and accepted by you, it is binding and cannot be changed by either party. Thus, if you accept an offer and are later contacted by a more-preferred site, you cannot renege on your agreement with the original site.

7 FREQUENTLY ASKED QUESTIONS FROM PROSPECTIVE INTERNS

This workbook was originally written as a resource to accompany an internship workshop conducted yearly at the American Psychological Association (APA) annual convention. We have conducted internship workshops at least annually since 2000. At each workshop, prospective interns have asked excellent questions about each aspect of the internship application and selection process. The questions posed and addressed in this chapter are representative of the common questions asked over the years at past workshops and include common queries submitted to Association of Psychology Postdoctoral and Internship Centers (APPIC) and American Psychological Association of Graduate Students (APAGS) representatives during the application and selection periods.

These questions are organized according to the chapter in which the specific application tasks are reviewed and related issues are discussed. The answers are composite responses that we consider good advice. As with any advice, you should consider these comments along with your own good judgment and the feedback you have received from your director of clinical training (DCT) in making a final decision about what course of action best suits your circumstances.

GETTING STARTED   *Question 1. How important is it for me to attend an APA-accredited or APPIC-member internship program?*

First, it is important to mention that some excellent internship programs are accredited and/or APPIC members and some excellent programs that are neither accredited nor APPIC members. Historically, many students have attended nonaccredited and non–APPIC-member programs each year and encountered no problems in their future licensing and employment activities.

http://dx.doi.org/10.1037/0000102-007
Internships in Psychology: The APAGS Workbook for Writing Successful Applications and Finding the Right Fit, Fourth Edition, by C. Williams-Nickelson, M. J. Prinstein, and W. G. Keilin

However, it is vital to understand that, as outlined in Chapter 1, the accreditation landscape is rapidly changing. Even now, APPIC often hears from those who attended nonaccredited programs who encounter substantial difficulties with the quality of their training, their ability to get licensed as psychologists, and/or their ability to secure suitable employment. Moving forward, it appears that accreditation will soon be the standard for all psychology education and training, and students from nonaccredited programs could experience significantly greater career difficulties in the future.

When considering internship programs, students need to be aware of the requirements of three entities: (a) their doctoral programs, (b) future licensing boards, and (c) future employers.

- *Regarding your doctoral program:* Many doctoral programs require an accredited internship to meet graduation requirements. It is important to check with your DCT to be sure that you understand what your program requires.
- *Regarding licensing:* Although many students each year complete nonaccredited internships and experience few, if any, difficulties when applying for licensure, you should be aware of the potential risks associated with nonaccredited internships. A few states or provinces may require an accredited internship and/or doctoral program to qualify for licensure. Some licensing boards require additional documentation, or in some cases, additional coursework, for applicants without an accredited internship. Some boards may deny you a license if your internship doesn't meet its criteria. This issue can get especially tricky if you do not know the specific state or province in which you intend to practice and thus cannot anticipate the future requirements that you will need to meet. The website of the Association of State and Provincial Psychology Boards (http://www.asppb. org) can be helpful in learning about licensure and in locating information about the requirements of various states and provinces.
- *Regarding future employers:* Some employers, such as Veterans Affairs facilities, require the completion of an APA-accredited internship and doctoral program to qualify for employment as a psychologist. Other employers may not have such a strict requirement, although some job and postdoc announcements do specify that an APA-accredited internship is a preferred qualification. Again, because it is difficult to know what your future career plans may be, it is advisable to check with your DCT and as many potential employers as possible to make an educated decision.

In general, there is no "right" answer as to whether one should consider attending a nonaccredited and/or non–APPIC-member internship program. Attending an accredited program is certainly the safest option, as you almost certainly will not have to justify the quality of your internship to anyone in the future. In addition, it provides you, in effect, with a seal of approval regarding the quality of training that you will receive and makes it unlikely that your internship program will be a barrier to licensure and/or future employment. Attending an APPIC-member internship that is not accredited does increase the risk to some extent, particularly for licensure boards or employers that require an accredited internship. Attending a nonaccredited, non–APPIC-member internship incurs the most risk, given that no external body has reviewed the site to ensure that it meets established standards of quality and given the potential risks to future licensure and employment opportunities.

The decision as to whether to attend a nonaccredited or non–APPIC-member internship program can be a difficult one, particularly if you are geographically restricted or are attempting to find an internship via the Phase II of the Match or the Post-Match Vacancy Service. We encourage you to consult with faculty or other knowledgeable individuals to carefully consider your career interests and options and to familiarize yourself with issues related to licensure and future employment.

Question 2. What if I learn that an internship program is planning to apply, or is in the process of applying, for APPIC membership and/or APA/CPA accreditation?

A site may have the best of intentions, but you should be aware that the application and/or approval processes for initial accreditation and/or APPIC membership could take far longer (even months or years longer) than a program anticipates. There is no guarantee that a program will ultimately attain accreditation and/or APPIC membership or will do so in a timely manner. Thus, although a program's training staff may convey confidence that they will ultimately be successful in the application process, such confidence may or may not be warranted, and you should consider attending such a program only if you clearly understand the risks in doing so.

Question 3. Is it possible to create my own internship site (e.g., by approaching an agency that doesn't have an established internship program and asking them to hire me for a year as an "intern")?

In answering this question, it is important to state that the predoctoral internship year is considered to be far more than simply a year of "work experience." For example, APPIC's current membership criteria state that a psychology internship "is an organized training program which, in contrast to supervised experience or on-the-job training, is designed to provide the intern with a planned, programmed sequence of training experiences" (see https://www.appic.org/Joining-APPIC/Members/Internship-Membership-Criteria). APA and many licensing boards have similar expectations for the internship experience. Creating one's own "internship" almost never meets, or even comes close to, the standards and expectations of these organizations.

So, although it is possible to create your own internship, doing so can jeopardize the quality of the training that you will receive and (as discussed earlier) carries substantial risks with respect to future licensing and employment opportunities. It is also something that most doctoral programs would not permit. We generally do not recommend this approach unless you are certain that it will be acceptable to your doctoral program, licensing board, and future employers.

Question 4. If I get placed at a nonaccredited internship program, is it acceptable for me to apply for and attend an accredited internship in the future? In other words, is it acceptable to attend two internships?

Although no specific rules prohibit the completion of a second internship, this is truly a bad idea. A nonaccredited internship should not be used as an opportunity to gain additional experience to qualify for an accredited internship. Also, once you have attended an internship, it is highly unlikely that another program would be willing to accept you for a second internship, particularly when there are many applicants who have difficulty securing their first internship. You should keep the following points in mind.

- If you are looking to gain additional experience to make yourself a more attractive applicant to accredited internship programs, then you should complete additional practica rather than a nonaccredited internship.
- Give very careful consideration to whether you want to attend an accredited internship. If you decide that you definitely want to attend an accredited internship, then you should not apply to or rank any nonaccredited programs, as doing so could result in your being placed at a nonaccredited program.
- A small number of doctoral programs will allow their students to graduate without an internship, and students in these programs sometimes pursue this option with the intent of completing an internship in the future. However, these students may not realize that the internship is designed to be completed while the student is matriculating through her or his doctoral program. As such, APPIC policies require a student to be enrolled in a doctoral program to be eligible for participation in the Match, and students who graduate before completing their internships may lose their eligibility to participate in future APPIC Matches.

Question 5. What are some ways for me to learn about the selection process and the APPIC Match?

We recommend that students begin learning about the selection process and APPIC Match as early in the process as possible. In particular, students should review the information located at two websites: APPIC (http://www.appic.org) and National Matching Services, Inc. (NMS; http://www.natmatch.com/psychint).

In addition, all applicants should subscribe to the APPIC e-mail list Match-News that provides news and information about the Match directly from APPIC. Match-News is a low-volume list, which means that you will typically receive only a few e-mail messages per month. A second APPIC e-mail list, Intern-Network, is a discussion list on which current and former intern applicants, some internship training directors, and APPIC board members discuss various aspects of the selection process.

All applicants are strongly encouraged to subscribe to Match-News early in the process; participation in the Intern-Network discussion list is optional.

Question 6. I have some fairly specialized interests and am looking for an internship that will meet these needs. How do I find such an internship?

First, check the *APPIC Directory Online* to see if the existing search options will allow you to locate an internship that meets your needs. If not, consider submitting an inquiry to the Intern-Network e-mail list to see if anyone can point you in the right direction. You also might try locating psychologists who are practicing in your area of interest (e.g., through professional organizations or e-mail lists) to see if they have any ideas about internship programs that specialize in this area.

Question 7. I carefully recorded my clinical hours over the past several years, but now I realize that I neglected to document the specifics about one of my brief training experiences. How do I go about estimating my hours?

Documentation of clinical experience typically requires students to report two kinds of information: (a) data about the actual hours spent in professional practice activities and (b) data on the personal characteristics of the clients served in those professional activities. Estimating the data about contact hours may be a simple process if you have a good idea of the number of clients you saw each week. From that bit of data, you can extrapolate and generate a good estimate of contact hours over the course of a training experience. Because professionals develop "habits of practice," a proportion of indirect clinical contact to direct contact more than likely is consistent across training experiences. Hence, if you completed 3 hours of indirect service for every 1 hour of direct service in other experiences, chances are good that you engaged in the same kind of clinical balance in this brief training experience.

Estimating the personal characteristics of clientele is more challenging. Referencing the general client data from your training site may be of help. Many sites collect aggregate service data for each month of each year; these data may help remind you about clients you served during that training period. Although it is possible to estimate these important bits of data, no amount of postexperience research or guessing will replace good record keeping during your training.

Most important, because your DCT is required to sign off on your practicum hours, it is important to discuss with him or her your methods of calculating your hours to ensure that they meet with the DCT's approval.

Question 8. I've had some unique experiences and am confused about how to document them on the APPIC Application for Psychology Internships (AAPI). How do I determine where on the AAPI they should be placed? Similarly, can I include my relevant work experience during my graduate program in my practicum hours?

The first step is to carefully read the instructions that are included with the AAPI, as this is where APPIC has addressed many of the most frequently asked questions about the application.

In general, keep the following points in mind when attempting to document your hours:

- If an experience appears to fall in more than one AAPI category or does not quite fit into any AAPI category, just use your best judgment to select the category that best captures the experience. Do not obsess or worry about it; there is often not a "right" way to classify certain experiences on the AAPI, so just use your judgment about how to document those hours.
- When the exact number of practicum hours or clients seen is not available, your best estimate of these hours is acceptable.
- If you are unsure about how to classify a particular aspect of your experience, consult with your DCT. In addition to being a good resource to answer this type

of question, your DCT must ultimately approve of how you have documented your experience on the AAPI.

- You may include relevant work experience obtained during your graduate program as part of your practicum hours only if your program considers this experience "program sanctioned."
- You may also contact APPIC if you have any questions about completing the AAPI. Contact information is provided in the AAPI instructions.

GOALS AND ESSAYS

Question 9. How personal do I get in the autobiographical essay?

This question is difficult to answer because every person has a different definition of "personal" information. Some essay readers may like to see some details about a prospective intern's personal (e.g., childhood) experiences, but others may find this information irrelevant. Maybe the best answer here is embedded in the preponderance of the comments that internship faculty make about this essay. That is, when internship faculty comment on pitfalls in autobiographical essays, they usually focus on those that are "too personal" rather than those that were not revealing enough. "Too personal" usually relates to discussion of numerous difficult life experiences that have shaped a student's life or to the disclosure of a great deal of personal information that does not necessarily relate to a prospective intern's professional development. On the other hand, some sites argue that students' essays are often not personal enough. Given this anecdotal information, it may be wise to present a balanced view of your personal experiences and to link those experiences directly to your professional development.

Question 10. I am sacrificing some of my goals so that I can complete internship in my immediate geographic region. How do I write my essays to communicate "fit" and be authentic at the same time?

This question suggests that personal values and goals are interfacing with professional values and goals. We believe that striving for that kind of balance is a good approach to the application and selection process. Achieving that balance may be difficult in a selection system that is characterized by "matching" training goals with opportunities. Our belief, however, is that most internship sites offer diverse, quality training experiences that will benefit students and promote their development. Thus, we contend that each internship has something good to offer, and just because it is close to home, its quality should not be discounted. By identifying your goals and values and objectively linking those to the opportunities afforded, you may realize that the "site next door" actually is a good fit and will promote your development. Hence, you can remain local and be "authentic" about fit.

CVS AND REFERENCES

Question 11. 1 have seen curricula vitae (CVs) that include personal information such as age, marital status, number of children, citizenship, place of birth, and so forth. Any insights about whether selection committees expect or want this information on applicants' CVs would be appreciated.

Our recommendation is to not include such information. Having that information on a CV is definitely not an expectation of selection committees, and the vast majority of applicants do not include it.

Question 12. Even though I can only submit three references per site, I can ask more than three references to write recommendations using the Standardized Recommendation Form (SRF) in case I want to send a certain supervisor's recommendation to a specific site. How common is it for applicants to ask for more than three letters and to send a lot of different SRFs to different sites? In other words, will I be at a disadvantage if I only ask for three references and use them for all the sites to which I am applying?

There is no clear agreement about this. Many people think that three letters are sufficient and may be used for all your sites, especially because you are likely to be choosing sites that all fit with your training goals. With this logic, you should not need overly-customized letters for different sites.

Conversely, a few people think having an additional SRF or two could not hurt if you are in a situation where you want to do everything possible to put your best foot forward to a program for which you desperately wish to be matched. Some students worry that not all the references will actually follow through and write their SRFs for you by the deadline. We hope the latter is not a typical situation, but we understand that this is a possibility. In either case, it certainly does not hurt to have an extra SRF or two available to use at your discretion with different applications. Keep in mind, though, that you cannot view the content of the SRF. You can only see the name of the reference and if it is complete. Sometimes, however, references will offer you a copy of their SRF, which is their prerogative. If this happens to you, it might be worth considering strategically aligning certain references to certain sites.

Recommendation letters are very important, but you should not overthink the process or try to be so tactical in your approach that you lose sight of the big picture. The advantages of obtaining an extra reference is that you are protected if one does not get completed by the deadline or if you really want different references for different sites. On the other hand, you might want to be sensitive about overloading your supervisors with reference requests. After all, having an extra letter requires that one other person take the time to write a letter for you.

The bottom line is that this question has no right answer. We suggest that you consider either just the number of references needed, or at most, one more.

Question 13. Once I have submitted my applications, when can I expect to hear back from sites?

The APPIC Match policies require sites to list their interview notification dates (the dates by which these programs are required to notify applicants as to whether they received an interview) in the *APPIC Directory Online*. Although APPIC recommends that sites adopt a December 15 interview notification date, sites are in fact free to set their own timelines. APPIC instituted this policy several years ago to make it easier for applicants to construct their travel itineraries.

If you have not heard from a site by the end of the day on its designated interview notification date, you may wish to contact the site (e.g., via phone or e-mail) the next day or soon thereafter to inquire about your status. In this situation, you may also wish to use APPIC's informal Problem Consultation and Resolution service to confidentially let APPIC know that a site didn't meet its obligation to notify applicants by its published interview notification date.

Question 14. Group interviews seem to bring out my competitive spirit. How do I go about "competing" without appearing overly competitive and defensive?

Interviews provide internship faculty with considerable information about applicants' interpersonal skills and coping resources. "Competitiveness" typically is not what faculty are looking for because they may infer that this competitive spirit will cause problems with other interns over the course of a training year. Therefore, we encourage you to approach these interview situations with "getting along" rather than "winning the slot" as your number one goal; if you get along with people, you have a better chance of winning the slot. Remember also that the individuals that you interview alongside will be your future colleagues throughout your professional life. It may be in your best interest to learn from, interact well with, and make a good impression on your colleagues, as well.

Question 15. Will I have to interpret a Rorschach on my interviews?

We do not have hard data on this issue, but anecdotal information suggests that very few sites and internship faculty require students to demonstrate specific skills during interviews. That is, rarely will you be handed a Rorschach protocol or an SPSS printout and be asked to "interpret this." However, you may be asked to present an example of a client with whom you have worked or conceptualize cases based on a handful of "facts," or you may be presented a clinical scenario that requires you to comment on how you would use your multicultural competence to address client needs. Be sure to practice a brief case presentation before you leave for your interviews.

Question 16. What can I expect to happen after the interview? Will sites stay in contact with me?

Again, contact varies significantly depending on the internship program. Some sites will have no further contact with you after the interview process is over, whereas others may contact you if they have additional questions or to give you an opportunity to ask questions of them. You really should not try to infer much about a site's interest in you based on how much postinterview contact they do or do not initiate—it really depends on their own approach to the process.

And, as emphasized in Chapter 6, any inferences that you may make about sites' interest in you should not in any way affect how you rank those sites. Remember that your rankings for the Match should be based only on your true preferences and should not be influenced by what you perceive as the likelihood that you will be matched to any site.

Question 17. What if I have questions for a site—maybe about their program, or whether they have received my application? Is it OK to contact them? If so, what is the best way to do so?

Many students hesitate to contact sites to ask questions about the program, application procedures, timelines, and so on, for fear of bothering the training director and negatively affecting their application. However, we encourage you to contact a site directly whenever you have questions. The *APPIC Directory Online* lists the ways in which a site prefers to be contacted (e.g., telephone, e-mail). Most training directors are eager to have you know as much about their program as possible—remember, they are trying to put their best face forward also. One caveat: Review the program's website and/or brochure, as well as their *APPIC Directory Online* information, before contacting a site, as it is best not to ask questions that are already answered in their materials.

In addition, one of the best ways to find out about a site is to talk with the current interns directly. Interns are often more likely to give you a balanced perspective about the internship experience at the site, including strengths and weaknesses of the program. Training directors understand that applicants like to talk with their current interns and will be happy to arrange for you to talk with one of them.

You also should remember that every contact that you have with a site could potentially be a part of the interview process. Even your interactions with support staff—positive or negative—might find their way to the selection committee. Sometimes current interns are members of the selection committee, and thus your contacts with them might ultimately be a part of the interview process as well.

Question 18. What should I do if someone at an internship site violates the Match policies by asking me about how I intend to rank that site?

We hope that this will not happen to you, as most training directors are very careful and do not want to put internship applicants in such an uncomfortable position (nor do they want to get into trouble with APPIC!). But if this does happen, the best approach is to politely remind the interviewer that the APPIC Match policies do not permit you to share such information with him or her. Of course, this can result in a brief uncomfortable moment in the interview and possibly some embarrassment on the part of the interviewer, but it can provide an important reminder to the interviewer about the policies. And, in most instances, the interviewer will gain respect for you for having the courage to appropriately set this boundary during an interview. Most of the time, such policy violations are the result of mistakes, misunderstandings, or miscommunications among the training staff, and rarely are intentional or malicious acts.

You should also remember that APPIC has both an informal problem resolution process and a formal complaint process that can be used to address violations of the Match policies. Thus, you should not hesitate to contact APPIC if you need assistance in resolving a difficult situation.

Question 19. What should I do if someone at an internship site asks me a question on an interview that is illegal?

According to an APPIC newsletter article by Mona Koppel Mitnick, Esq., an attorney and the public member of the APPIC Board of Directors, the following questions should not be asked of internship applicants unless they relate to actual qualifications for the position or the applicant raises the issue himself or herself: marital or family status, religion, physical condition or limitations, sexual preference, or physical or mental health status. This is not an exhaustive list, and there may be certain conditions in which some of these questions may be legally asked.

If you are asked such a question during an interview, there are a couple of ways to respond. One approach is to let the interviewer know that you are not comfortable answering the question or that you believe that it is not an appropriate question for an interview. However, we do recognize that some applicants may be hesitant to respond this way out of concern that it will lead to a negative response by the interviewer or that they will be seen as resistant or uncooperative.

Another approach is to simply answer the question in the moment but to take some form of action at a later time. For example, you could later (either after the interview or after the entire selection process) contact the training director to inform him or her that you were asked a question that you believe may be illegal. Our belief is that most training directors will be grateful that you have brought this issue to their attention so that they can take corrective action with the individual involved.

Alternatively, you can use APPIC's informal problem resolution or formal complaint processes to address the situation. In particular, if you are unsure about the legality or appropriateness of a particular interview question, the informal problem resolution process can provide an opportunity for you to discuss the situation confidentially with an APPIC representative and review the options that might be available to you.

Also, keep in mind that you may consider some interview questions to be inappropriate but that are legal nonetheless. A good example is, "Tell us about the other sites to which you have applied for an internship." Some applicants find this question to be somewhat intrusive and unnecessary, but nothing prevents a site from asking it.

Additional resources on the topic of legal and illegal interview questions may be found at the APPIC website (http://www.appic.org).

THE MATCH

Question 20. When should I register for the Match? What happens if I register late and do not get my applicant code number in time to provide it to sites on the AAPI?

Although APPIC recommends that all applicants register by December 1, we generally recommend that you register for the Match in September or early October to receive your applicant code number and include it on the AAPI. However, if you are unsure about whether you will be applying for internship in the coming year, you may wish to wait until closer to the deadline, as the Match registration fee is nonrefundable and nontransferable to a future year. If you register later in the process, don't worry—simply enter it into the AAPI Online once you do receive it.

Question 21. Both my partner and I will be applying for psychology internships this year. Are there any special procedures that are available for us?

Any two applicants who wish to coordinate their choices of internship may participate in the Match as a "couple." Most couples will find it advantageous to use these special procedures to attempt to secure internships in the same geographic area. More information is available on the APPIC and NMS websites.

Question 22. What considerations do I use when constructing my rankings?

The most important thing to remember is to simply rank internship programs in the order in which you want them. That is all you need to worry about. Do not, under any circumstances, take into account such things as how you believe a site is ranking you, how well you think you have impressed a site, the feedback that you are getting from a site, and so forth. The matching program has been specifically designed to allow you to rank sites in the order in which you want them, without consideration of these other factors, to be assured of receiving the best match possible.

Question 23. What if I do not know whether I am still under consideration by a site? Should I still rank that site?

As long as you are still interested in the site, you should rank it. It does not hurt you in any way to rank a site that does not ultimately rank you. If that happens, the computer will simply skip over that site on your list and proceed with the next ranked site, without having reduced your chances of being matched to any other site on your list.

Question 24. I am hesitant to give up my top ranking to a site that does not seem all that interested in me.

This is an understandable concern, but it is not something that you need to be concerned about. If a site is truly your top choice, then you should absolutely, positively rank that site as number one on your list regardless of how interested in you they seem. By doing so, you will not have reduced your chances of being matched to other sites on your list if your top-ranked site does not work out.

Question 25. I just received a letter today from one of my ranked sites stating that I was no longer under consideration. But I have already submitted my rankings! Any suggestions?

Not to worry: The computer will simply skip over that program on your list—it will not affect your chances of getting matched to any of your other sites. In other words, even if you did log in to the Rank Order List Input and Confirmation system to remove that program from your list, it would not matter—You would still be matched to the exact same program as if you had left it on your list.

Question 26. Given my current circumstances, I am not completely sure that I want to attend internship during the coming year. Should I still submit a rank order list (ROL)?

You should submit an ROL only if you are absolutely, positively, 100% sure that you are ready to accept the internship to which you are matched. The APPIC Match is binding, and you are not permitted to change your mind once matched to an internship site. Thus, if you are unsure about your ability to commit to internship during the coming year, then you should not submit an ROL.

Question 27. What if I decide that I do not like the internship site to which I have been matched? Is it possible to change my mind?

No, you are required to attend the internship program to which you are matched. Thus, if a program is not an acceptable option for you, you should not include it on your ROL.

Question 28. What is the first thing that I should do if I am not matched to an internship site in Phase I of the Match?

First, remember that you still have an opportunity to apply for internship positions in Phase II of the Match and the Post-Match Vacancy Service. Second, talk with people. Talking with your significant others will give you the support you need and some guidance about how to proceed. Talking with your academic advisor and your DCT will help you identify the necessary steps to search for available internship slots that are acceptable to you and to important others in your life. Be sure to review the material in this workbook (Chapter 6) that discusses Phase II and the APPIC Post-Match Vacancy Service, along with the extensive instructions and suggestions for applicants located on the APPIC website.

Question 29. I think that a site may have violated an APPIC policy. I am uncertain if their behavior was really a violation, and even if it was, whether I should risk reporting it. What should I do?

Probably the best approach is to discuss the situation with APPIC's Informal Problem Consultation representative (see http://www.appic.org and click on "Problem Consultation" for contact information for this person). Your initial contact with this consultant will be to confidentially discuss the situation and is an opportunity for you to better understand your options for resolution of the problem. Contacting APPIC does not obligate you to take any action or to file a complaint.

The Match policies were put into place to make the internship application and Match process one that is fair and respectful for students and sites alike. Although violations are uncommon, they do occur. Students often wonder whether reporting a potential violation will have negative consequences for them or their chances of securing an internship. This is rarely the case. Your situation can be handled informally or formally, depending on the nature of your complaint. If the problem is serious, it is important for you to inform APPIC of the problem because one of their member sites may not be complying with the rules it agreed to abide by.

Question 30. I would like to consider doing an internship in another country. Is this possible? What should I be aware of or concerned about?

This has become a much more complicated question in recent years, given the political tensions regarding issues such as immigration and terrorism. Below are some issues to consider.

- Completing an internship outside of the United States or Canada is extremely difficult to do successfully. APA, the Canadian Psychological Association (CPA), and APPIC do not recognize programs in other countries, and thus any training experience outside of the United States and Canada will be, by definition, non-accredited. Furthermore, educational standards can be very different in other countries, and locating an internship program that is acceptable to a U.S. or Canadian licensing board can be extraordinarily difficult.

- Each year, about a dozen students from Canadian schools match to U.S. internship programs, and a similar number of students from U.S. schools match to Canadian programs. In recent years, APPIC has received a number of reports of students being turned away at the U.S.–Canadian border when attempting to cross for internship, and some were never able to attend their internship despite the involvement of immigration attorneys.
- Students who attend an internship accredited by CPA, but who plan to eventually work in the United States, may find that CPA accreditation does not carry the same weight or credibility in the United States as does APA accreditation. The same may hold true for students who attend APA-accredited internship with plans to move to Canada for employment. CPA and APA are engaging in efforts to increase mutual recognition, but this is very much a work in progress.
- The laws and rules of some jurisdictions may deprioritize noncitizens when it comes to competitive hiring processes.

Question 31. I have more questions that have not been addressed in this chapter. What do I do?

You have several options available. First, ask your DCT or other faculty members for assistance. You may also contact Dr. Greg Keilin directly via e-mail (gkeilin@mail. utexas.edu) or telephone, (512) 410-0002, and he will be happy to assist you.

8 ADVICE FOR DIRECTORS OF CLINICAL TRAINING OF STUDENTS IN THE INTERNSHIP APPLICATION PROCESS

As a director of clinical training (DCT), you already are aware that the students in your program applying for internship likely are experiencing a significant amount of anxiety related to the application process. To some extent, this anxiety is normative and adaptive. Although there are now sufficient sites for every applicant, an imbalance remains between accredited internship sites and the number of students applying. Moreover, students become quite attached to their top choices and remain extremely nervous they will not get their preferred site, or any of the sites on their list within Match Phase 1. Remember, data still indicate that over three quarters of students do match in Phase I, and almost half of all students who match receive an offer from their first-choice site. These statistics have been relatively consistent for many years, and your students previously have been quite successful when participating in very competitive application processes (i.e., applying to doctoral programs in professional psychology).

Your job as DCT, in large part, is to help your students manage their anxiety as much as possible. However, you may be able to help your students prepare a strong application and be optimally prepared for the rigorous application process in several specific ways. This chapter outlines a series of specific strategies that may be useful for you when advising students in your program. The application process also has changed significantly over the past several years. Several of these changes also are discussed below.

STEP 1. ORIENTING STUDENTS TO THE APPLICATION PROCESS

Most application deadlines are at the end of October through late November in the academic year of the Match. Several months earlier, your students likely will begin to peruse the online directory of internship programs (http://www.appic.org). The summer

http://dx.doi.org/10.1037/0000102-008
Internships in Psychology: The APAGS Workbook for Writing Successful Applications and Finding the Right Fit, Fourth Edition, by C. Williams-Nickelson, M. J. Prinstein, and W. G. Keilin
Copyright © 2019 by the American Psychological Association. All rights reserved.

is often a good time for a general meeting with your students. During this meeting, you may want to inform them of several points listed below.

- A good first step for the applicant in this process is to determine his or her training goals for the internship year and beyond. These goals can help guide an applicant through each stage of the process (i.e., selecting sites, writing essays, answering interview questions, ranking sites) and will help the applicant remain focused and grounded for the next several months. See Chapter 3 for more information on setting training goals.
- The *APPIC Directory Online* is updated in the spring of each year. It is important to visit the site periodically and to use both broad and narrow searches to help capture sites that may be the best fit for their training needs.
- It is important to immediately subscribe to APPIC's Match-News e-mail list for important updates throughout the process. The Intern-Network e-mail discussion list may also be of interest to some, but it often increases anxiety for many who eavesdrop on very detailed conversations and questions among other applicants.
- You may wish to share a list of sites that are common among students in your program. Students tend to be most successful when applying to sites that are familiar with your doctoral program and have previously selected your students as successful interns.
- Remind students that they will need to complete the application process at the same time as other program requirements. Many students report that the internship process takes as much time and energy as would one find in a moderately intensive graduate course during the fall semester; students are mostly unavailable (physically or psychologically) for the month of January; and many students find their productivity waning between February and June. It is best to plan for these time commitments early.
- Many students appreciate a timeline with suggested deadlines (see Exhibit 8.1).

Exhibit 8.1.　*Internship Application Timeline*

Deadline	Task
September 1	Construct (almost) final list of sites to which you are applying (15 maximum).
September 20	Compute clinical hours.
	Update curriculum vitae.
	Order transcripts.
	Select and notify faculty who will write you letters of recommendation.
	Register for the Match.
	Make list of supplemental materials or special requirements needed for each application.
October 10	Complete first draft of essays.
October 20	Complete final draft of essays.
	Make sure all letters of recommendation have been submitted to the online application portal.
October 25	Begin process of uploading and routing all application materials online.

A Reframe

In addition to a review of these application-related tasks, your first meeting with students also may include a reframe on the internship application process. Many of your students will enter this process with a single goal: to match. But the process they are about to undertake actually offers much more.

The internship application process is an outstanding professional development opportunity. Rarely do our students get a chance to reflect on their experiences; review their career goals; and think about how they are a unique, autonomous, and efficacious psychologist. Many students also have a narrow vision of the workplace for psychologists, simply because they have had substantial exposure to only one model of psychological research and practice (i.e., in your program). This process, if taken seriously, will change that. The essays are self-reflective exercises. If they do the essays well, students learn a great deal about themselves while writing (and rewriting) them. The interviews are a "world tour" of the field, the many settings and roles of psychologists within it, and an opportunity for social networking that will likely be relevant to their professional experiences well beyond the internship year. The internship application process is another educational experience in the progression of experiences that students get in doctoral training. Like all other educational experiences in your program, this one can be overseen by you and your faculty in a way that helps students get the most out of it.

To facilitate your students' professional development, use your meeting at the start of the process to ask your students questions, such as the ones below.

- Where would you like to be professionally in 5 to 10 years? What specific skills/ experiences do you need to get from where you are today to where you want to be?
- Imagine that another student in this program had the exact same research, practica, and didactic experiences as you, on paper. What makes you different from that other student? Think beyond what training you had and contemplate your reactions, impressions, observations, and reflections to each training experience.
- What do you think is important in the field? What contribution do you want to make?
- How do your beliefs about your research area differ from those of your research advisor? How do your ideas about clinical work differ from those of your clinical supervisor?

When students have truly contemplated these types of questions, you will notice a substantial improvement in the quality of their essays and in their responses to mock interview questions. Challenging them to continually think of these issues at the start of the application process also will help them gain an educational experience that will endure, whether they match.

STEP 2: HELPING STUDENTS COMPLETE THEIR APPLICATIONS

Although many of your students will be able to complete most parts of the application autonomously, it is not a bad idea to take a quick look at each part of their application. In particular, many students have little experience with preparing a formal curriculum vitae (CV) before this stage in their career. Carefully reviewing and proofreading their

CV can be extremely helpful for them. It may be useful to circulate the CVs of prior students who applied to internship to help folks understand how prior graduate experiences from your program traditionally are documented on a CV.

Similarly, many students have questions about how to calculate their hours. You should familiarize yourself with the general instructions for calculating hours by reviewing suggestions online (http://www.appic.org) and by reviewing the instructions in the Association of Psychology Postdoctoral and Internship Centers (APPIC) Application for Psychology Internships (AAPI) Online itself (note that it is perfectly acceptable for you to create a free AAPI Online account so you can see its functionality firsthand). If you are unable to answer a question from a student about how certain hours are to be counted, you may contact the AAPI Online coordinator (see the "Contact" page on the APPIC website for contact information).

A quick review of students' list of sites also can be enormously helpful. It is critical that students know not to apply to a limited geographic area, if at all possible, because this is one of the strongest predictors of being unmatched. It also is important to make sure that students apply to a reasonable number of places (between 10 and 15) and to remind them that at least a few of them should be sites where your program has placed interns before.

It is a good idea to review each student's list of references. Although little empirical data are available regarding the factors in a letter of recommendation that are associated with positive internship outcomes (particularly since the vast majority of recommendation letters are uniformly glowing), some evidence suggests that letters predominantly from outside the formal graduate program or from references who do not have doctoral training in psychology, or conversely, letters missing from one's primary mentor can raise concerns among internship selection committees.

Essays

Once students reach the internship application process, most of the content in their application is no longer malleable. Their clinical hours and CV-related experiences already are accrued. Their references' professional impressions largely have been formed. Their transcripts can no longer be improved meaningfully. However, students still can substantially influence their outcome by working conscientiously and thoughtfully on their essays, and as DCT, you can be a tremendous help to them in this process.

In this workbook, we have offered substantial suggestions, guidelines, and directions for successfully completing the essays that are part of the internship application process. In addition to reviewing these suggestions, some more several specific ways in which you can help students create effective essays are described below.

1. Do students' essays help distinguish them as a unique psychologist? It is quite common for students to write essays with a broad statement of experiences and interests. Often, students have not challenged themselves to think of their expertise as valid, unique, and distinct. Your encouragement and feedback, from the perspective of a training director who can identify unique strengths of each student's training, can help students to communicate a clear identity in their essays that will help them seem unique and interesting to the selection committee.

2. Do students describe their accomplishments too modestly in their essays? Our professional culture does not involve self-promotional skills, at least as much as is seen in some other professions. In fact, psychology trainees often are plagued by "impostor syndrome" and uncertainty regarding their own skills. The internship application process requires some sales ability, however. You may be surprised how often students neglect to include prestigious honors in their autobiographical statement! As one who reads many applications (for graduate school admissions), you are very aware that such important selling points often need to be repeated in more than one place in one's materials to catch the attention of a bleary-eyed reviewer.

3. Are students' training goals realistic? Many students have accrued substantial exposure to a university-based clinical service system during graduate school but have not yet learned what other types of clinical experiences may be available at an internship setting. By reviewing their goals and helping students express them clearly, and repeatedly, throughout their essays, you will help your students to communicate a match to each training program.

4. Does the autobiographical statement seem too familiar? Commonly, a student's autobiographical statement reads like the story of why he or she chose graduate school in professional psychology—perhaps similar in tone and content to what you read years ago when this student first applied to your program. It is far more important for this essay to tell the story that started with graduate school admission, ending with the rationale for specific internship training goals. Because all students applying for internship have somehow found their way to the profession of psychology and successfully gained entry into a doctoral program, that part of the story is typically not relevant or helpful in establishing a distinct identity as a psychologist. An autobiographical statement that helps the internship committee identify unique graduate-level skills, accomplishments, and interests is more useful at this stage. Also, keep in mind that some sites may want students to include autobiographical details that are not necessarily professionally relevant. Advise students on the level of personal detail that feels appropriate and offer feedback to students that helps them develop an essay that is uniquely theirs (i.e., that clearly conveys their personality and interests).

5. Do essays read like term papers? The second and third essays in the internship application process ask about case conceptualization/orientation and multiculturalism/diversity, respectively. Students' responses to these questions often read like a final exam from a graduate course. Although this may communicate a strong knowledge base, such a style does not help to differentiate the applicant from others who have had graduate training. Help your students express their opinions and unique viewpoints in response to these questions. A potential supervisor likely will be most enthusiastic about an applicant who will be stimulating in supervision. These essays can be used to help communicate such a quality.

6. Last, are the "fit" arguments in the cover letter and essays compelling? From your experience reading hundreds of applications, you already know what works in an essay. As with graduate student applicants, intern applicants also need to communicate enthusiasm and a well-thought-out rationale for wanting X training at Y site.

Interviews are happening earlier and earlier each year; some are scheduled for the first week in December. It is best to meet with intern applicants and prepare them for "interview season" as early as possible.

First, it is probably very important to inform students that applicants will hear from internship sites at very different times over the months of November and December. Even interview invitations from the same site can reach your students weeks apart. It will be important for them to resist the temptation to compare themselves to others. Fellow applicants' news has no bearing on the news they may soon receive.

The process of scheduling intern applicants into available interview dates has turned lately into a subtle form of guerilla warfare. Program assistants seem to call applicants earlier and earlier, sometimes asking for schedule commitments on the spot, and without much patience, grace, or understanding of the complexities from the applicants' perspective. To be sure, scheduling is complex and hectic on both ends of the process, and the competition on all sides has become more intense. As a result, students often become quite rattled and hesitant when attempting to negotiate the complexities of scheduling. You can be an excellent sounding board for these students by offering feedback on whether their concerns and requests are appropriate, professional, and communicated adequately.

As DCT, you surely will want to discuss the protocol you wish your students to follow should they have to reschedule, cancel, or decline an interview. The behavior of this year's applicants may affect the success of next year's applicants to a given site. From a program perspective, you may wish to offer clear guidance on how you want applicants to handle such situations.

Although this can be quite difficult, this also is a good time to sit down with an applicant from your program who you suspect may not navigate the interview process successfully. Internship sites increasingly look toward doctoral programs and their DCTs as the gatekeepers for the profession. If you do have a student whose social skills, attire, or professional presentation contributes to a suboptimal first impression, it is very useful to counsel that student accordingly before he or she moves on to the interview stage of this process.

Many doctoral programs provide substantial support during the application process but considerably less for the internship interviews—usually because they assume that students who receive interviews will ultimately be successful in securing a position. However, it is not at all uncommon for a highly qualified student to get many interview offers because of a well-written application, only to have a disappointing Match result due to poor interviewing skills. As DCT, it is imperative to remember that the competencies that make a student a wonderful researcher, teacher, or clinician are very different from the competencies required to be an effective interviewee. Thus, even your best students may need substantial assistance with the interview process.

Regardless of their past success in your program, then, all students can benefit from a brief role play with you before their first interview. The interview role play offers an excellent (a) exposure exercise to reduce anxiety; (b) confidence-building exercise, as students typically realize that interviewing is something they already know how to do well; (c) rehearsal for answers to commonly asked questions; and (d) opportunity for feedback, including students' self-evaluation, along with your evaluation of their interview behavior.